The Overflowing Life

The Overflowing Life

CLARENCE W. CRANFORD

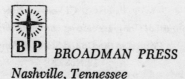

BROADMAN PRESS

Nashville, Tennessee

422–207

DEWEY DECIMAL CLASSIFICATION: 248
Library of Congress catalog card number: 64–12409
Printed in the United States of America
12.N63KSP

Contents

CONTENTS

Introduction

In her book of stories about Maine, Sarah Orne Jewett speaks of trees that seem to grow right out of bare rock. "There's sometimes a good hearty tree growin' right out of the bare rock, out o' some crack that just holds the roots," she says, "right on the pitch o' one o' them bare stony hills where you can't seem to see a wheel-barrowful o' good earth in a place, but that tree'll keep a green top in the driest summer." Then she gives the explanation. "You lay your ear down to the ground an' you'll hear a little stream runnin'. Every such tree has got its own livin' spring." And she adds, "There's folks made to match 'em." [1]

How to grow to spiritual maturity out of the rocky barrenness of a materially minded culture—that is our problem. We live in an age of urbanization, mechanization, industrialization, specialization, militarization, and nuclearization. These are important aspects of our contemporary world but hardly the soil out of which to grow a rich, satisfying spiritual life. Every soul must have access to a flowing spring if it is to live and grow.

Jesus spoke of such a spring in his promise to a woman of Samaria. At Jacob's well, he said, "Whosoever drinketh of this water shall thirst again: But whosoever drinketh of the water that I shall give him shall never thirst; but the water that I shall give him shall be in him a well of water springing up into everlasting life" (John 4:13-14).

7

Wonderful words, but what do they mean? It is obvious that the Christian experience was never meant to be a temporary blessing like a spring shower that waters the earth briefly and then passes away. Rather, the Christian life should be an ever-flowing spring that continues to refresh the soul.

This ever-flowing spring should lead to an overflowing life. Every vital experience waits to be shared. Suppose, suggests Robert McAfee Brown, you get 100 on an algebra test, or you get a good summer job, or you fall in love. What happens? You have a joy that you want to share with someone else. You are not necessarily boastful, but you have to let your joy "spill over" to someone else.[2]

But suppose, he goes on to say, something even more wonderful has happened to you. You have had a lot of puzzling questions about the meaning of life, and suddenly you have an experience that seems to clear them up. You experienced a bitter tragedy, but you felt you were not alone for God was with you. Sooner or later you discover that you want to share with others the good news that life makes sense, that God is real, that you are not alone. These are things that one simply cannot keep quiet about once he knows they are true.

This was the psalmist's experience. Life brought him face-to-face with enemies and dark valleys, but there was something more. Life also confronted him with experiences and blessings that made him feel that there is a great Shepherd who knows how to lead to green pastures and protect in the midst of the shadows. So, as the psalmist considered his blessings, he wrote, "My cup runneth over." As he fed in the green pastures and drank of the still waters of God's love, his became an overflowing faith.

Wherever Jesus went, his faith and love overflowed in compassion and power. Children were aware of his tenderness as he blessed them. Sick people felt the overflow of his power when he touched them. Social outcasts knew the overflow of his redemptive concern as he ate and talked with them. Even when his sense of truth and justice overflowed in words of righteous indignation, love was the source of his anger.

The same overflow of courage and conviction was seen in the disciples after Pentecost. Empowered by the fact of the resurrection, they went forth to declare the message of him "whom God hath raised up, having loosed the pains of death" (Acts 2:24), and to preach "through Jesus the resurrection from the dead (Acts 4:2). When some of the leaders who had been responsible for Jesus' death saw the boldness of John and Peter, they "took knowledge of them, that they had been with Jesus" (Acts 4:13).

Compare this with the cautious, colorless discipleship of so many today, and ask why the difference. Instead of being like a stream that deepens and widens as it flows, many Christians give the impression that their Christian experience is like a shallow pool from which much of the joy and enthusiasm has evaporated. Their commitment is casual and costless. Their discipleship is listless and lukewarm. Instead of a song, the Christian life to them has become an old story.

Some people, of course, do not want an overflowing faith. They want a faith that speaks to their own personal needs, especially in times of crisis, but not one that flows out in radiant witness. They can be enthusiastic about food, politics, sports, or hobbies, but concerning religious faith they are silent and uncommunicative.

Even in the churches, the discipleship of many members is shallow and weak. Yet in every church, there are those whose faith stands out as evidence of a deep and abiding trust. Instead of being a burden, the Christian life for them is a source of strength. Instead of a dull habit, the Christian life is a vital way of life.

How does one experience this abundance of faith and power? How does one sense the goodness and guidance of

God so that it overflows in Christian love and power? This is our quest as we seek to know more about the overflowing life —a quest that will bring us back repeatedly to him who promises us thirst-quenching faith. If we turn to the world for refreshment, it will leave our deep thirst for meaning in life unsatisfied. If we try to satisfy our thirst by loyalty to the church without first drinking of the love that flows from Calvary, we shall thirst again. If we limit our search for spiritual renewal to the support of a favorite pastor, we shall thirst again. Only as we discover the eternal springs of God's forgiveness and love pouring through the life and death of Christ can our thirst be truly satisfied. He leads us to the deep, hidden springs of spiritual power which flow beneath the rock-hidden soil of our materially minded culture.

1. The Overflowing Life

In our quest of the overflowing life, let us first take a new look at an old psalm. Let us enter again the experience of one who could say with such a glad heart, "My cup runneth over."

There is a sense of excitement and adventure about blazing a new trail or exploring an unfamiliar road to see where it leads. The world is indebted to those bold explorers and thinkers who have dared to strike out into the unknown. An amazing world of science and invention has opened up because men have not been afraid to explore the new. There will always be those venturesome persons who will risk their lives to climb an unscaled mountain just "because it's there." There will always be those adventurous souls who will hear and respond to the call:

> Something hidden. Go and find it.
> Go and look behind the Ranges—
> Something lost behind the Ranges.
> Lost and waiting for you. Go! [1]
>
> RUDYARD KIPLING

There is also a deep sense of satisfaction in walking down an old path where one is familiar with every twist and turn. Every tree and stone is an old friend. One knows just when and where certain flowers will bloom; what birds will call along the way. Even there, no two experiences of walking along the same path are ever identical. Always some new dis-

11

covery, some new delight awaits the questing mind, the alert and appreciative spirit. There may be some new flower to catch one's eye, some new combination of light and shadow to delight one's fancy. A study of art can cause one to see beauty in familiar places where it had not been noticed before. An increased knowledge of science can help one to see designs in nature which had been previously missed. Some new light, some new shadow, some new experience, some new mood, some new inner need can make the most familiar path take on new meaning as one walks along it.

The danger, of course, is that what to a child would be an adventure filled with new and exciting discoveries will, to one long familiar with the way, become just an old story—just a necessary means of getting to a desired destination. One looks at familiar objects without really seeing them. He has seen them so often that they fail to register their uniqueness and beauty on his mind. The beauty of a flower makes little or no impression. The bird's song goes unnoticed. One's mind is on other things.

So it can be with the twenty-third Psalm. To most people this psalm is like an old, familiar path down which they have strolled hundreds of times. They know its every phrase and illustration. They revel in its portrayal of the Good Shepherd. They delight in its promise of green pastures and still waters. They turn to it for comfort and assurance in time of sorrow.

In fact, they know the psalm so well, that their very familiarity with it may cause them to fail to look for new and deeper meanings in its well-known lines. And yet, if one approaches it right, one never seems to catch all the lights and shadows of its meaning. At any rereading, some new insight, some new understanding may be revealed in a way one has not fully appreciated before. A word, a phrase over which one has skimmed hundreds of times may suddenly shine with new brilliance. One may, hundreds of times, for example, have read the familiar line, "Yea, though I walk through the valley of the shadow of death," without ever really catching the full significance of the important preposition "through." He may have read it with no more discernment than if the psalmist had merely said, "Yea, though I walk *into* the valley of the shadow." But one day it dawns on the delighted reader that the word is not just "into"; it is "through." "Yea, though I walk *through* the valley of the shadow." Death is not a stopping place. The psalmist is saying that death is a passageway into a larger experience. Henceforth, this little preposition stands out as one of the truly big words in the psalm as it gives added assurance that death is a journey through a shadowy vale into God's eternal sunlight on the other side.

Or, one's attention may suddenly be drawn with new insight to the word "shadow" in the same sentence. It is not just "the valley of death" but "the valley of the *shadow* of death." A shadow can frighten, but it cannot hurt us. Children can so easily be frightened by shadows. But shadows lose their power to frighten if one's father is with him. As the little boy said, when he was asked to put the empty milk bottles out on the porch, "It's too dark to go out there tonight without a father." When his father stepped out on the porch, however, the boy lost his fear of the darkness. He walked out on the porch as confidently as if it were daylight.

Many people are so familiar with the promises of this psalm, they fail to see its challenges. They do not see how much faith it takes to say, "The Lord is my Shepherd; I shall not want." Most people prefer to trust science and industry to fulfil their wants. What wants have they that man's ingenuity and adequate income cannot provide? They prefer the securities of this world to the adventure of trusting in God. Man, rather than God, has become the real object of their trust.

Nor do they see the implications of being led "in the paths of righteousness." If we have walked too swiftly past that verse, we need to go back and take another look at it. For this verse has significant implications for our behavior. It makes tremendous moral and ethical demands upon us. This makes the psalm much more than just a source of comfort in time of sorrow. It makes it a call to righteousness—God's kind of righteousness—a way that calls for dedication, discipline, and courage. If we have thought that the central thought of this psalm is expressed in the phrase, "lie down," we had better look again. We are fed by green pastures and are allowed to drink from still waters that we may walk "in paths of righteousness" along which God himself leads us.

But the righteousness of which the psalmist speaks is not just an unwilling submission to authority or conformity to law. It is the overflow of a full and grateful heart. The psalmist's desire to follow the shepherd is a natural consequence of one who can say, "My cup runneth over." This is why Theodore Wedel defines Christian ethics as "gratitude ethics." But this is the basis of all biblical morality and ethics. The author of Exodus does not preface the Ten Commandments with an injunction to obey them because they are right. He begins by calling attention to God's providence. He begins by saying, "I am the Lord thy God, which have brought thee out of the land of Egypt, out of the house of bondage" (Ex. 20:2). Then follows the giving of the Ten Commandments. They are to be obeyed as a result of gratitude for the amazing providence of God.

Obviously, the psalmist's use of an overflowing cup is a reference to God's unfailing and unlimited providence. But it is more than that. It is description of a life that is full to overflowing. Overflowing with what? Overflowing to what? These are important questions. How to find a faith that overflows into proper, vital action is both our problem and our need. In the psalm certain of these questions are answered. Read in the light of the total psalm, this verse makes the psalm of the Good Shepherd also the psalm of the overflowing life.

How seldom one sees a life that seems to overflow with real spiritual power. How few give evidence of an overflowing sense of gratitude for old blessings or eager anticipation for new ones to come. How few can say that they face each day with what Margueritte Bro calls "something of the day-before-Christmas feeling we had as children." How few give evidence of deep inner resources that light up their lives and give an added quality to their work, or deserve the tribute paid to Andrew Peabody on the walls of the Harvard Chapel: "He walked among the professors and students of Harvard for thirty-six years, and wist not that his face did shine." [2]

Albert W. Beaven once defined evangelism as "the overflow of our enthusiasm for Jesus Christ." Perhaps that is why there is so little genuine evangelism in so many of our churches today. There is so little real enthusiasm for Jesus Christ and his way of life. Churches overflow with a desire to succeed in worldly terms. They overflow with a desire to get new members, especially from those of good standing in the community. But how many overflow with a genuine desire to share Jesus' spirit, love, and obedience to the divine will? We have changed Paul's witness, "Woe is unto me, if I preach not the gospel" (1 Cor. 9:16), to "Woe is unto me, if my church interferes with my pleasures." We have changed his ringing, courageous declaration, "I am not ashamed of the gospel" (Rom. 1:16), to "I hesitate to mention it, for one does not want to seem fanatical about this sort of thing, but I do get a lot of comfort out of believing the gospel."

Instead of faith in God being like a cup running over, most people give the impression that the cup of their spiritual blessings is only partly filled, if not almost empty. In fact, millions seem to be interested only in the dregs at the bottom

of life's cup. Reversing Moses' dedicated stand, they prefer
the pleasures of sin for a season rather than to suffer for
righteousness' sake with the people of God. Although such suffering overflows with manifold blessings for the world, and in
the lives of those who suffer, most people refuse to suffer for
Christ's sake.

Many of our reasons for failing to see faith in God as an overflowing blessing are made clear by the psalm itself. The psalmist's overflow came from an overwhelming awareness of the
grace and guidance of God. "He maketh me to lie down in
green pastures: he leadeth me beside the still waters. He restoreth my soul: he leadeth me in the paths of righteousness
for his name's sake." It is God who provides. It is God who
leads. Man's role is gratefully to receive and follow.

But this is strange language to modern ears. We are not ac-
customed to hearing, "Trust in the Lord with all thine heart;
and lean not unto thine own understanding. In all thy ways
acknowledge him, and he shall direct thy paths" (Prov. 3:5-6).
With us it is "better things for better living through chemistry."
We do not boast, "The heavens declare the glory of God; and
the firmament sheweth his handywork" (Psalm 19:1), but
"Astronaut orbits the earth."

As for the rod of his protection, even that does not seem
quite so necessary in a country like the United States where no
one is persecuted for his practice of religion. Why do we
need God's protecting rod? The state will protect us. The
policeman in front of the church is there to direct traffic,
not to spy on those who are entering the church.

Moreover, we so often drive a wedge between the sacred
and the secular, between work and worship, between prayers
and pleasures, between the clergy and the laity. Religion for so
many people is a cup from which they sip a little inspiration
at an occasional church service as a spiritual pick-me-up to
offset the weariness and meaninglessness of overindulgent

living. But this is a far cry from what Jesus meant when he asked the disciples, "Can ye drink of the cup that I drink of?" (Mark 10:38). One does not drink of that cup merely by going to church but by giving one's self unreservedly to do God's will in the world whatever the cost.

Admittedly, some things are religious and some things are worldly, and like oil and water they do not mix. But to say that a man is religious at his worship but not his work, at his prayers but not his pleasures, is to overlook God's lordship over *all* of life. After all, grass is material stuff. Green pastures have to do with agriculture and economics. Jesus himself taught us to pray for "daily bread." God is as interested in economics as in theology. He wants us to work toward a world in which every one will have enough to eat.

Science and industry are not God's competitors. They must never be elevated to where they become our graven images. They cannot take God's place. But properly conceived and used, they are expressions of his goodness. They are part of the way he today prepares a table before us and anoints our head with oil. Therefore, he is as interested in what we do at our workbench as in what we do in church. As Brother Lawrence contended, to pick up a straw from a littered floor can be a service to his glory. Or as a more modern writer has put it:

> There are strange ways of serving God;
> You sweep a room or turn a sod,
> And suddenly, to your surprise,
> You hear the whirr of seraphim,
> And find you're under God's own eyes,
> And building palaces for Him.[3]
>
> HERMANN HAGEDORN

The overflowing life, then, begins with a great faith in God, not as a vague, impersonal something, but as a vital, personal, compassionate someone. "*He* maketh me." "*He* leadeth me." "*He* restoreth my soul." "*He*." "*He*." As William Adams Brown has put it, "God may be more than person; he may be other than person; he cannot be less than person. No word that is less than personality can so fittingly suggest what our experience of his working shows him to be." [4] In the words of Martin Buber, God is *Thou*, not *It*.[5] And he leads us like a shepherd. A present-day teacher has suggested that in our industrial age it would present a more familiar picture to say, "The Lord is my engineer." But that would destroy the very thing the psalmist wanted to convey about God. One can hardly say of an engineer, "He shall carry his blueprints in his bosom," but it makes sense to say of God, "He shall feed his flock like a shepherd: he shall gather the lambs with his arm, and carry them in his bosom" (Isa. 40:11). One may never have actually seen a shepherd, and yet the concept of the shepherd stands as a symbol of tenderness and compassion even in our industrialized society. The figure is consistent with the way in which God's nature—that for which his name stands—is revealed by his works to men.

For God, as the psalmist reminds us, is a God who *acts*. He *makes*. He *leads*. He *restores*. He *protects*. Everything he does is consistent with himself and with his divine purpose for mankind. He leads us in the paths of righteousness "for his name's sake." He leads us in the paths of righteousness because he himself is righteous. John R. Sampey used to say, "God cannot tell a lie, because that would be contrary to his nature."

God leads us in the paths of righteousness because that is in keeping with his nature. God is not whimsical; he is righteous. As Abraham insisted, "Shall not the Judge of all the earth do right?" (Gen. 18:25). He is not vindictive but redemptive. "He restoreth my soul." The great agony of God's heart, as Isaiah saw so clearly (5:7), is that having made the world, "he looked for judgment, but behold oppression; for righteousness, but behold a cry" (of the oppressed).

Isaiah also saw with prophetic clarity that if man's situation were to change for the better, God himself must be involved in the answer; God himself must suffer in the transaction. The Shepherd, so to speak, must become as a lamb that is led to the slaughter and as a sheep that "before her shearers is dumb" (53:7). He must accept suffering for the sake of the world he would redeem. Perfect goodness is not enough. Righteousness alone cannot prevail. Man who rejects God's goodness must experience God's mercy. Only then can his heart be melted and become as a cup running over with awe, adoration, and joy at the goodness and mercy of God that follow him all the days of his life and promise to continue even into eternity itself.

This is why John 10 must be added to Psalm 23 to complete the picture. God will do nothing that is contrary to his nature, and his nature is forever and fully revealed in the person and work of him who said, "I am the good shepherd: the good shepherd giveth his life for the sheep" (John 10:11). Thus the cross becomes God's staff as he reaches out in love and pain to draw us back into the shelter of his fold.

Let the cynic say, "Science is my shepherd; I shall not want. It maketh me to lie down on foam rubber mattresses." The person who wants his life to overflow with peace and power will say from the depths of a grateful heart, "The Lord is my shepherd; I shall not want. He maketh me to lie down in green pastures: he leadeth me beside the still waters. He restoreth my soul." And he does it all because that is the kind of a God he is. He comes with compassion. He leads with righteousness. He restores with mercy. He can do no other and be true to himself.

2. The Yoke of Discipline

After the death of Blaise Pascal, famous seventeenth-century French mathematician and religious thinker, there was found sewed inside his coat like an amulet words which he had written at the time of his initial Christian experience: "Certainty, joy, certainty, feeling, sight, joy, joy, joy, tears of joy." [1] Strange words to come from a committed scientist. They show that some experiences cannot be measured in cold, mathematical terms. Pascal had evidently had a mystical experience of no small dimensions. God had certainly filled his heart to overflowing. That this was no mere ephemeral mood with him is shown by his subsequent life and writings as he continued to combine his genius as a mathematician with an unusual sensitivity to the presence of God.

Not everyone is stirred to such emotional rapture, or states it in such ecstatic language. But whoever has felt the assurance of God's love, and has tasted of the still waters of his mercy, knows a heart overflowing with gratitude, wonder, peace, and joy, and is conscious of an intensified sense of love and moral victory. Indeed, this is one of the evidences of the reality of God's presence in one's life—that he begins to know victory where before he had known defeat, and his faith begins to overflow in a higher quality of character and conduct. Bernard of Clairvaux could write:

I confess that the word has visited me, even very often. But although he has frequently entered my soul, I have never at any moment been sensible of the precise moment of his coming. By what means he has made entrance or departure I confess I know not to this day. . . . How could I then know that he was present? . . . Only by the stirring of my heart was I enabled to recognize his presence, only by the amendment of vices and the strong restraint put upon all carnal affections did I know the might of his power.[2]

He knew that someone with cleansing power had visited his heart, because he found it a cleaner and neater place. How else can we know that one's cup is full except as it overflows in purer love and nobler action?

Whether one knows the initial rapture of Pascal or the quieter sense of indwelling of Bernard of Clairvaux, the important thing is how to keep the initial experience of God continuing and vital. The author of Lamentations says of the Lord, "His compassions fail not. They are new every morning" (3:22–23). How to keep alive our awareness of this abundance; how to keep our cup raised to receive his offering; how, as Moffatt translates Paul's injunction to the Romans, to "maintain the spiritual glow" (12:11)—this is our problem. To continue overflowing, one's cup must be replenished. This, too, God has promised to do.

Jesus said, "Whosoever drinketh of the water that I shall give him shall never thirst; but the water that I shall give him shall be in him a well of water springing up into everlasting life" (John 4:14). He promises to keep our cup full to overflowing because the supply of his love is never failing, but we must continue to hold the cup. However rapturous the first refreshing taste, we must not think we can drain its contents in one gulp. Conversion is the beginning, not the end of religion. When asked if he did not think that conversion was the end of religion, J. O. Williams replied, "Yes, the front end." To change the figure, all the grass is not at the edge of the pasture. Or as Paul put it, God means for us to go on "from strength to strength."

Yet it is so easy, once we have been refreshed, to be con-

tent with our spiritual beginning, rather than to want to follow
the Good Shepherd up the grassy slopes. When we are
tempted, as we so often are, to wander from the paths of
righteousness, or to lag behind, instead of moving forward at
the sound of the shepherd's voice, we need the staff of discipline to draw us back and pull us on. Here, perhaps, the
New Testament figure of the yoke is better than the staff. God
could use the staff of his power to draw us against our will, but
each person must decide for himself whether he wishes to be
yoked in loyalty and obedience to Christ. Since Jesus himself
used the figure of the yoke, it may be well for us to move from
the figure of the staff to that of the yoke as a symbol of
discipline and obedience.

The world today is yoked to vast forces of materialism, nationalism, and militarism. These forces are running away with
it. Unless something happens to prevent them, they may drag
us to our destruction. To a world yoked to such destructive
forces, the voice of Jesus comes today to say, as it did to those
who were yoked to a slavish obedience to the Mosaic law with
all of its later ridiculous amplifications, "Take my yoke upon
you, and learn of me; for I am meek and lowly in heart:
and ye shall find rest unto your souls. For my yoke is easy,
and my burden is light" (Matt. 11:29–30).

It was Elton Trueblood who, a few years ago, suggested a
new emphasis on the yoke as a Christian symbol. If the cross
stands as a symbol of Christ's sacrifice and redemptive love for
us, the yoke stands as a symbol of our obedience and discipleship to him. To be yoked to Christ is to be led in the way
he goes. It is to be led forward in our Christian experience. It
is to serve with him. It is to be obedient to his commands. It is
to accept discipline as a means of continued fellowship with
him.

Assuming the awareness and glad acceptance of God's love
as the beginning, there can be no continued spiritual growth

without discipline. This would seem to be obvious, yet, among so many Christians, blandly ignored. The road to anything worthwhile is still restricted and narrow. The scholar knows he must accept the discipline of arduous study to master his subject. The artist knows he must practice his art. When asked how he could draw such perfect circles with a freehand stroke, Holman Hunt replied, "You must practice eight hours a day for forty years, and then it is just as easy as this." The surgeon knows that his skill depends on practice. Dr. Chevalier Jackson, the great Philadelphia surgeon, spent hundreds of hours when he was otherwise relaxing, learning to tie knots inside a matchbox with one hand. A college athlete who ran the hundred-yard dash had difficulty getting off smoothly at the start of a race. He set himself to the task of practicing the getaway ten thousand times until he had trained his nerves to respond automatically to the crack of the starter's gun. Discipline we know in other realms, yet there is so little of it in the average Christian's life.

Moreover, discipline must be practiced on a regular basis. The musician who practices only when he feels like it will never become a great artist. The author who writes only when he feels in the mood for it will probably never finish his manuscript. Yet many Christians seem to think that they should read the Bible, pray, and go to church only when they feel like it. Most writers learn that they must hold themselves to a rigorous schedule in which they try to turn out so many words a day. Often in the course of maintaining their schedule, the inspiration comes, and frequently they find they have done some of their best work when they felt least like beginning it.

So it is with prayer. Margueritte Bro says, "In almost any skill allied to science, art, or plain old living, it is every day that counts. Prayer grows in meaning as we grow in practice." [3] Speaking for some of the more experienced persons in prayer, she says, "The very regularity of our period of devotion works for us . . . inducing the mood and quality of devotion." [4] Not that periods of devotions spell the whole of discipline in any Christian's life, or that man by discipline can claim God's love or force his mercy. "By grace are ye saved through faith; and that not of yourselves: it is the gift of God: Not of works, lest any man should boast" (Eph. 2:8–9). But neither can he experience spiritual progress without it.

This is not to suggest that inspiration runs on schedule. The entire *Magic Flute* Quintet is said to have occurred to Mozart while he was playing billiards. He did not work for his inspiration; it was given to him. At least, Mozart's genius and a person's desire to pray have this in common. Pascal contended that one could not have a craving for that which he had never tasted. If we desire to know God in prayer, it is because he has already planted the desire in our hearts. This does not mean we cannot cultivate the art of prayer—indeed we must. Nor does it mean that every experience of prayer will be equally rewarding. Some may be very disappointing.

Convinced that Christian lives could be revitalized by the regular practice of certain Christian disciplines, and that Christian churches could be transformed if groups within them would seriously practice such disciplines, Elton Trueblood formed what he called the "yokefellow" fellowship. It was made up of those who would voluntarily promise to maintain certain regular disciplines as an aid in realizing and maintaining a continuing sense of the presence of God. There is nothing new about the disciplines he suggests. They are the same expressions of discipleship and means of cultivating a sense of the presence of God that Christians have always known they should practice, but so few really do. The disciplines suggested for the "yokefellow" movement are:

1. *The Discipline of Prayer.*
    To pray every day, preferably at the beginning of the day.

2. *The Discipline of Scripture.*
    To read reverently and thoughtfully, every day, a portion of Scripture, following a definite plan.
3. *The Discipline of Worship.*
    To share, at least once a week, in the public worship of God.
4. *The Discipline of Money.*
    To give a definite portion of my annual income to the promotion of the Christian cause.
5. *The Discipline of Time.*
    To devote a specific portion of my time to ministering to the needs of others.
6. *The Discipline of Work.*
    To strive to make my daily work a Christian vocation.
7. *The Discipline of Study.*
    To develop my mental powers by careful reading and study.[5]

It cannot be said too strongly that such devotional practices do not take the place of a life fully surrendered to God. A few minutes spent in Bible reading and prayer are no substitute for a whole life lived to his glory. One cannot say, "There, I have had my visit with God for today. Now I can go about my work and forget him until this time tomorrow." The best way to keep one's mind focused on God in times of prayer, as Brother Lawrence pointed out, is "not to let it wander too far at other times."[6] The only way to keep sincerity in one's devotional life is to keep God central in all of life. Nels F. S. Ferré reminds us, "worship is not only the occasional standing on holy ground but the constant living on it."[7]

It is now possible to put a drop of a chemical on a snowflake that will form around it and harden into a plastic coating. The plastic is sufficiently porous that eventually the water of the snowflake evaporates leaving only the empty form. The shape of the snowflake is retained. The snowflake itself is gone. So any act of worship becomes an empty form if we lose a true love for God, if we lose the desire to know and to do his will. How to avoid the peril of vain repetition, on the one hand, and the neglect of prayer, on the other, is the

Christian's problem. It is a good habit to pray, but prayer, or any devotional practice, should never become a thing of mere habit. No pattern of discipline should become so set and standardized that it loses its power to motivate life. A set time in the day is not the only time one can talk with God. Brother Lawrence, who went so much further than most of us in the practice of the presence of God, warns, "Do not always scrupulously confine yourself to certain rules, or particular forms of devotion, but act with a general confidence in God, with love and humility." [8]

In fact, the yoke of discipline is not something we can slip on and off at will. When we accept the yoke of Christ, we accept it as a symbol of obedience in everything. Everything is brought under his rule that we may be guided in the way of life, that "in all things" he may have the pre-eminence.

Nor, in the light of God's gifts, is this an unreasonable thing for him to ask. A certain agnostic professor in a leading American university seems to take great delight in pointing out what he considers parallels between the teachings of Jesus in the New Testament and the demands of Hitler in *Mein Kampf*. Evidently, he makes no attempt to differentiate between the moral qualities of the two persons and the movement each sought to initiate. Perhaps, claiming to have no belief in God, he has no basis for judging the difference. Even the most untutored mind should be able to distinguish between the orders of a tyrant and the commandments of the great Teacher, unless, of course, he has no true basis for evaluating what is right and wrong. To compare the demands of Hitler with those of Jesus is like seeing no difference between a gunman saying, "Hands up," and a mother saying, "Hold out your hands so that I can see if you have washed them." Both are commands, but what a difference in motivation and purpose. One violates another's rights. The other seeks to promote another's welfare.

There are two kinds of obedience: servile and creative. The first is the kind demanded by a dictator. The second is the kind required by a wise and loving parent. The dictator demands allegiance as a show of power; the parent requires it as a means of guidance. One is prompted by arrogance and lust for power; the other is prompted by love. The parent is not mean to his child when he insists that he stop playing with a knife. He is trying to protect the child he loves until the child has achieved enough experience and maturity to handle this danger for himself.

Moreover, it makes all the difference in the world whether one speaks from a podium of hate or from a cross. Guy Bowden points out that "the realization that He who has the right to exact our obedience has stooped to ask for it, prevents that obedience becoming a grudging, unwilling submission to an authority imposed from without." [9] God demands our obedience as a father, not as a tyrant. He does not shout, he whispers. He speaks through him who "came not to be ministered unto, but to minister, and to give his life a ransom for many" (Matt. 20:28). Compared to those who set the world's standards and demand our conformity, Jesus can say, "I am meek and lowly in heart" (Matt. 11:29). Compared to the burdens of the world with its ever increasing weight of materialism, militarism, and sensualism, Jesus can say, "My yoke is easy, and my burden is light" (Matt. 11:30).

We must never forget that we are yoked to Christ in faith because he was first willing to be yoked to us in love. He put himself in our place and bore the yoke of obedience to God. By that obedience he revealed the perfect will of God. Jesus is still yoked to us in love. "Lo, I am with you alway, even unto the end of the world" (Matt. 28:20). To be yoked to Christ is to be yoked with him in the adventure of doing his work in the world. It is to be joined with him in fellowship and sharing, even the fellowship of suffering. He understands our suffering, because he himself suffered for us. It is this that makes us love him so, and it is love that makes the burden light.

Can Jesus' burden be light when he demands our entire allegiance? Is his burden light when he asks us to carry his message to the ends of the earth? Is his burden light when he asks us to take up our cross daily and follow him? Is his burden light when it requires that to be forgiven, we must be willing to forgive? Jesus asks it in love, and love makes the difference —his love for us and our love for him, and the love he generates in us toward others. It is the old story of the girl who was asked why she was carrying such a heavy baby, and who replied, "He's not heavy; he's my brother." The story may reflect too much maturity for a child, but the recognition of this truth is a mark of maturity in a Christian.

A grudging task lifts us up, even in the midst of our tiredness, when it is done in love. Whether we think of God's leading as a staff or a yoke, it is a staff and yoke of love. To know this is to love him for his watchcare over us. To love him turns discipline into joy, prayer into a privilege, his church into a channel of blessing, just as our love for another turns labor into a service of love. Thus we are able to run with patience the race that is set before us, looking unto him who for the joy that was set before him, endured the cross. And part of his joy came from obeying the Heavenly Father whom he loved.

3.
Exercises for
the Soul

Some years ago, Howard Arnold Walter wrote:

> I would be true, for there are those who trust me;
> I would be pure, for there are those who care;
> I would be strong, for there is much to suffer;
> I would be brave, for there is much to dare.

Strength to face life's tests and demands—Howard Walter recognized this as one of the basic needs of the soul. Indeed, the Bible itself calls on us to love God with all our heart, with all our soul, and with all our strength. The shepherd wants strong sheep. It delights his heart to see young lambs skip and gambol about the pastures, for he knows that by such play they are exercising young muscles and building strong bodies. How can their bodies overflow with energy if they are not strong? He wants sheep strong enough to follow him through desert stretches to new pastures, strong enough to follow him as he leads through drought-filled hours to fresh water. He does not want them to remain lambs, but to grow into strong, healthy sheep.

So also the Lord wants men of strong faith. But how can one's faith overflow in radiant witness if he does not exercise his spiritual powers? Just as physical exercise helps to build strong physical bodies, so spiritual exercise can help to build a stronger awareness of God.

No one has to tell a child to exercise. Nature fills him with such abundant energy, he can hardly keep still. As he grows older, he may need to give attention to the need for physical exercise, especially in these days of urban living and easy transportation. In former days, when there were fewer labor-saving devices and when life was more rural, the need for physical exercise, for most people, was no problem. But nowadays, when for millions of city dwellers physical activity is limited to walking between the parking lot or bus stop and the office, or at most guiding a power mower over a miniature lawn, or weeding a flower border, it becomes necessary to invent forms of physical exercise. Gymnasiums and golf courses must entice people who live sedentary lives to exercise their muscles.

A new Christian may feel like bounding for joy because God has entered his heart. But Christian stewardship may get to be an old story. Through neglect of prayer and worship, spiritual awareness may begin to atrophy. To prevent this, one needs the worship and fellowship of the church. He also needs to spend moments alone with God so that his heart will be ready when, as Peter expressed it, "the times of refreshing shall come from the presence of the Lord" (Acts 3:19). To this end, what might be called spiritual exercises can help as a means of toning up tired spiritual muscles and strengthening one's awareness of God.

The idea of spiritual exercises is not new. People have probably engaged in some form of spiritual exercise ever since men have believed in a Supreme Being. In the sixteenth century, Ignatius of Loyola, founder of the Jesuit order, perfected a set of spiritual exercises as a guide for penitence and prayer.

For as to go for a walk or a journey, and to run, are bodily exercises, so is the name of spiritual exercises applied to any method of preparing and disposing the soul to free itself from all inordinate affections, and after it has freed itself from them, to seek to find the will of God concerning the ordering of life for the salvation of the soul.[1]

The Protestant reader would reject the idea that any amount of spiritual exercise can contribute to the saving of the soul. This is a gift of God's mercy—one that no acts of ours can merit but may be received through faith. Nevertheless, spiritual exercises can help to strengthen one's spiritual perceptions and awareness of the presence of the living God. The modern text of Ignatius' *Spiritual Exercises* is still studied by those who want to find new spiritual vigor through guided meditation and prayer. Though they were undoubtedly written with monastery life in mind, they do contain many excellent suggestions for contemplation. They do remind us of the need to strengthen our spiritual perceptions by taking time for meditation and prayer.

Allan Knight Chalmers [2] has made suggestions, particularly to young people, of spiritual exercises that can help them to pray. Learning that the time spent in prayer by individuals in a Christian group averaged less than two minutes a day, he challenged them to save up their two minutes a day and at the end of the week spend fifteen minutes, a half hour, or an hour or more in uninterrupted meditation and prayer.

Because he knew they had not learned the art of listening and meditation and might not know how to use such an extended period for prayer, he suggested several ways in which they could keep their mind focused on God for the period. He suggested, for example, that in the privacy of their own rooms, they might hold their arms extended as they thought of the cross. When their arms began to ache and became so heavy they must drop them to their sides, they could meditate on the fact that they were just beginning to understand something of the agony through which Jesus was willing to go for the redemption of the world. They could then thank God for Jesus' willingness to suffer for our sakes.

The fingers of one hand could suggest four persons for whom to pray, while the fingers of the other hand might suggest four problems about which to pray. As the persons and problems are remembered in prayer, the fingers could be closed in the form of a fist. As the thumb came around the fingers, it could remind the individual of how the Spirit of God surrounds our lives and of the biblically stated truth that we are "bound in the bundle of life with the Lord" (1 Sam. 25:29).

Many writers on prayer, such as Frank Laubach, for example, have suggested similar exercises.[3] Whether one reacts favorably or not to the use of physical means to help focus one's attention in prayer—and they are suggested only for those who feel the need of them—the thought of spiritual exercises in terms of guided meditation can help one to concentrate his thinking on God and can add to his awareness of the divine presence. First, however, it is necessary to say that there is one vital difference between physical exercise and spiritual exercise. In physical exercise one engages in increased activity. Spiritual exercise calls for the exact opposite. It calls for relaxation and stillness of soul as one listens to the inner voice.

It is only still waters from which sheep will drink. Because of their heavy wool, they instinctively fear turbulent waters. We, too, need to drink from the still waters of quiet waiting before the Lord. After a leisurely hike through Connecticut, Odell Shepard wrote of his experiences under the inspiring title, *The Harvest of a Quiet Eye*. That is what we are after in spiritual exercises—the sight of truth and meaning that becomes clear in moments of meditation that often elude us in the hustle and bustle of the everyday world.

This truth was recognized by the psalmist. Jerusalem was besieged by the Assyrians. The shouts of warriors, the thud of spears, the sounds of chariots and horses filled the ears of the people as the "heathen raged." It was a critical moment for Jerusalem. It was a time when the waters "roar and be troubled," and the mountains of danger shook "with the swelling thereof." Fortunately for the residents of Jerusalem, there was a water supply from the pool of Siloam, a stream that made "glad the city of God" (Psalm 46:3–4).

Then the Lord uttered his voice, and "the earth melted" (v. 6). Overnight the flower of the Assyrian army lay dead, slain by an invisible hand. Plague or miracle, it was providential for the city of Zion. In the stillness that followed the noise of battle, as the chariots left behind by fleeing Assyrians burned in the fire, the people had time to think. Now was the time for Israel to listen to the voice of God. Was the siege a judgment upon them? What must they do? How must they be changed to be worthy of the saving hand of God? And so, through the psalmist, the Lord spoke to the people to say, "Be still, and know that I am God" (v. 10).

Be still! What a difficult order to obey today. We are such activists it is difficult for us to be still even when we sit. Even silences in church services bother us. Something must be happening, someone must be speaking every minute, or we are ill at ease. We have lost the art of being still—of listening for and to the still, small voice. We are told the early Hawaiians spent long periods of meditation at their altars before approaching them to "breathe life" into their prayers. When the Christians came, their prayers were so short and so lacking in prior meditation, the white men were called "haolis," meaning "without breath," since they did not take time to "breathe life" into their prayers.[4]

Concerning our neglect of practicing the art of being still for creative thinking and communion with God, Samuel H. Miller says:

Although Moses entered the mountain, Jeremiah the potter's house, Jesus the wilderness, we in our time fear to waste time by such action. . . . Even when we pray, we are so verbal-minded, that we think we cannot commune with God except we busy ourselves with much speaking. . . . How great a skill it is to listen, so that in the quiet peace of the soul there can be heard the word of truth spoken for the first time, or the voice of the Eternal, that still, small voice, which is never heralded with trumpets or the mighty clamor of the mob.[5]

Thomas à Kempis called silence "the nutriment of devotion." Emily Herman says, "There is such a thing as a divine science of waiting . . . its master-key is silence." [6] "If the soul is to work," says Miller, "it must rest—if it is to speak, it must listen." [7]

Recognizing the need first to achieve a spirit of quietness and receptivity, let us carry out the analogy of exercises by suggesting a breathing exercise for the soul: *breathe in thoughts of the greatness, the goodness, and the mercy of God.*

First, we need to think of the greatness of God. Nels Ferré says, "We tend to treat God as though He were one of us." [8] We have forgotten that "the Lord he is God: it is he that hath made us, and not we ourselves; we are his people, and the sheep of his pasture" (Psalm 100:3). We approach the God of the universe as if it were a privilege for him to hear us, instead of marveling that he who "hath measured the waters in the hollow of his hand, and meted out heaven with the span, and comprehended the dust of the earth in a measure, and weighed the mountains in scales, and the hills in a balance" (Isa. 40:12), forever holds out the scepter of his love that we may always approach and be heard.

This is where Job began to find his answer. After the agony of his sorrow and the tortures of his illness that inevitably turned his thoughts in on himself, after the incessant arguments of his friends—why do people talk too much to one who is in sorrow when a firm handclasp or a brief word of love may say more eloquently what needs to be said?—Job's thoughts were drawn to the greatness of God. "Where wast thou when I laid the foundations of the earth?

declare, if thou hast understanding. Who hath laid the measures thereof, if thou knowest? or who hath stretched the line
upon it?" (Job 38:4–5). Job did not get definitive answers to
his questions, but he got more. He got a vision of God. Soon
he found himself saying, "I have heard of thee by the hearing
of the ear: but now mine eye seeth thee" (42:5).

Margueritte Bro says that "probably more of us are stirred to
the mood of prayer through reading the high thoughts of others than by any other single approach." [9] Where can we turn to
get such high thoughts of God as can be found in the Bible?
Here is the best way to breathe in thoughts of the greatness of
God. What a sense of awe and wonder greets one as he reads
Job 38 and 39 with the breath-taking review of the creative
activity of God. Where in all literature can one find a more
exalted concept of the magnitude of God's creative power?
Read again the inspiring fortieth chapter of Isaiah with its
similar panoramic survey of God's creative activity, asking its
great question, "To whom then will ye liken me, or shall I
be equal? saith the Holy One" (v. 25).

Or turn back to the incomparable stories of creation in
Genesis. Or see once more through the eye of Psalm 139 the
omnipresence of God: "Whither shall I go from thy spirit? or
whither shall I flee from thy presence? If I ascend up into
heaven, thou art there: if I make my bed in hell, behold, thou
art there. If I take the wings of the morning, and dwell in the
uttermost parts of the sea; even there shall thy hand lead me,
and thy right hand shall hold me" (vv. 7–10). These are but a
few of the innumerable passages of the Bible that lift us out
of our little, mundane world and fling us out into space where
we are brought face-to-face with the mystery of creation and
the power and might of the Creator.

Or turn to secular literature. Sidney Lanier, for example, is
led to think of the greatness of God as he contemplates his
beloved marshes of Glynn:

As the marsh-hen secretly builds on the watery sod,
Behold I will build me a nest on the greatness of God:
I will fly in the greatness of God as the marsh-hen flies
In the freedom that fills all the space 'twixt the marsh and the skies:
By so many roots as the marsh-grass sends in the sod
I will heartily lay me a-hold on the greatness of God:
Oh, like to the greatness of God is the greatness within
The range of the marshes, the liberal marshes of Glynn.[10]

Undoubtedly, the marshes of Glynn grew smaller as Sidney Lanier became more traveled, but his concept of God must have grown as his experience broadened. The world today has shrunk to a very small orb. Some people seem to think that God has shrunk with it. But the more man studies the universe, the more mystery he confronts, not less. Robert Oppenheimer writes of new particles streaming from smashed atoms and complains that they present "vast jumbles of new numbers, all with an insulting lack of obvious meaning." [11] It is in search of some "meaning" for it all that many scientists recognize the need of religion.

The amazing thing is that this God of the universe, this architect of stars and atoms, is not just a creator of cosmos. He has a shepherd's heart. He is concerned about people but not just about people in general. He is concerned about each individual person. Here is a thought with which to fill one's spiritual lungs. "When I consider thy heavens, the work of thy fingers, the moon and the stars, which thou hast ordained," said the psalmist, "What is man, that thou art mindful of him?" (Psalm 8:3–4). Jesus gave answer. "What man of you," he asked, "having an hundred sheep, if he lose one of them, doth not leave the ninety and nine in the wilderness, and go after that which is lost until he find it?" (Luke 15:4). If a shepherd would do so much, can we think God would do less? Man is not just an infinitesimal speck lost in the immensities of the stars. He is to God what the sheep is to a shepherd. The shepherd knows each sheep by name. "It is the nature of love," says D. T. Niles, "to individualize." [12] Jesus said, "It is not the will of your Father which is in heaven, that one of these little ones should perish" (Matt. 18:14).

This is the truth that becomes evident as we see God's love revealed in Jesus. To the critics who accused Galileo of pushing God out of the world by his new views of the universe, he answered, "The sun which has all those planets revolving about it and dependent on it for their orderly function can ripen a bunch of grapes as if it had nothing else in the world to do." [13] So Jesus who carried in his heart God's concern for the whole world, when he stands by Jacob's well, "talks with the woman from the village as if this was all that had to be done in the world." [14]

This, says Leslie D. Weatherhead, is part of the significance of Jesus' statement, "I am the door of the sheep." In the Near East, Weatherhead tells us, the shepherd is literally the door of the sheep. When he leads the flock to the fold, the shepherd stands in the doorway to inspect each sheep. When he has poured oil on its cuts and wounds, he steps aside to let it enter and steps back into the doorway to examine the next sheep.[15]

God never loses the individual in the masses. When asked whose son he was, a little boy, lost from his parents during a London air raid and unable to recall his name, sobbed, "I guess I ain't nobody's nothing." But to the God we see in Christ, a penitent thief on a cross was somebody's something. A cursing fisherman was worthy to be called to be a disciple. A despised tax collector was seen as worthy to write a gospel. And through faith in the gospel, common men and women became "kings and priests unto God." Oh, the goodness and mercy of God that he "who commanded the light to shine out of darkness, hath shined in our hearts, to give the light of the knowledge of the glory of God in the face of Jesus Christ" (2 Cor. 4:6).

The second exercise for the soul is a lifting exercise: *lift yourself and others up to God in prayer.*

A young man came to Washington, D. C., to study. He was brilliant and bitter. Bitter because an attack of polio in his infancy had left him a cripple. To try to overcome his bitterness, he began to read books on psychology. They helped him to analyze his bitterness but not to get rid of it. One day he met a person who seemed to have a radiant faith in God. When asked how he got such faith, this person replied, "Mostly through prayer." The young student began to drop into a nearby church for meditation and prayer. It didn't happen overnight, but as he opened his heart before God in prayer, a new spirit invaded his life. He became a radiant Christian, one who has been most helpful in guiding other students to a deeper faith in God.

But prayer does not stop with ourselves. It becomes a way by which we lift up others in faith before God. When someone is sick or in trouble, something in us makes us want to pray for them. That there are questions about praying for others, few would deny. How does God use our prayers? Certainly we are not asking God to conform to our wishes, or to violate another person's will. Yet, if God is God, and God is everywhere, what better way is there to express our faith in him and our love for others? Certainly Jesus prayed for others. To Simon Peter he said, "I have prayed for thee, that thy faith fail not" (Luke 22:32). "The Holy Spirit," says Frank Laubach, "is ever eager to break through, but fails, except where He finds loving, joyous, unity in prayer." [16]

We cannot do our best work in an atmosphere of suspicion and distrust. What if even the Holy Spirit cannot do his best work in an atmosphere completely devoid of our prayers? By prayer, we place our faith and love in God's hands to use, like the boy's lunch at the feeding of the multitude, in his wisdom for those for whom we have prayed. We help to contribute to a more creative situation in which his Spirit can work. After all, Jesus honored the faith of those who brought the man "sick of the palsy" to him. "When Jesus saw *their* faith, he said unto the sick of the palsy, Son, thy sins be forgiven thee" (Mark 2:5). He knew more than they where the real need lay, but they had faith that Jesus could heal if they bore their friend into his presence.

Prayer is not proved by argument but by practice. The way to sense the power of prayer is to pray. There is no substitute. Reading books on prayer can give us valuable hints and insights, but they cannot take the place of prayer. Nor can we wait until we have answered every question about prayer before we begin to pray. Sir Arthur S. Eddington, famous British physicist, once described what happens, scientifically speaking, when one steps through a doorway. He wrote:

I am standing on the threshold about to enter a room. It is a complicated business. In the first place I must shove against an atmosphere pressing with a force of fourteen pounds on every square inch of my body. I must make sure of landing on a plank travelling at twenty miles a second round the sun. . . . I must do this while hanging from a round planet headed outward into space. . . . The plank has no solidity of substance. To step on it is like stepping on a swarm of flies. . . . These are some of the difficulties. . . . It is necessary to determine in which direction the entrophy of the world is increasing in order to make sure that my passage over the threshold is an entrance, not an exit. Verily, it is easier for a camel to pass through the eye of a needle than for a scientific man to pass through a door. Whether the door be a barn door or church door, it might be wiser that he would consent to be an ordinary man and walk in rather than wait till all the difficulties involved in a really scientific ingress are resolved.[17]

So it is with prayer. We do not wait until we have argued the case of prayer *versus* natural law. We begin to pray for ourselves and others, and the God who has ordained that even we shall carry forward the work of the saints and the prophets, so that they "without us should not be made perfect" (Heb. 11:40), waits for our prayers as an evidence of our faith in him and our love for those for whom we pray. As Rufus Jones so beautifully puts it, "We are happy to believe and trust that our intercourse with the Companion of our lives has helped to fill with love the cup which some friend of ours with agonizing hands was holding up in some hour of need." [18]

The third spiritual exercise is a stretching exercise: *reach out in love to someone in need.* An American tourist was walking down a street in Hong Kong. A little, hungry Chinese girl had knelt down on the sidewalk to look at the food in a bakery store window. She was so tired, and had looked so long, she fell asleep with her little forehead pressed up against the glass window. It was such an appealing sight, the American took her picture. When he returned to the States and showed the picture, someone asked him, "What did you do after you had taken the picture?" The man said, "What can I say? I did not waken the little girl and buy her a loaf of bread. I just walked on photographing more need."

We do not have to go to Hong Kong to see human need. It is on the street where we live, in the same city, in the same state. Of course, there is tragic world need. Not all of it is physical need. Much of it is spiritual. Someone is weary of life. Someone is lonely. Someone is baffled by life. Someone feels unloved. A kind word that someone has gone out of his way to speak, a deserved compliment passed on, or a little deed of kindness can often make the difference between shadows and sunshine in someone's life. It will also leave an afterglow in the heart of the giver.

We were not meant to spend all our time on our knees in prayer. Prayer becomes a stimulus to action. We pray that God may stab us awake to human need as we begin to see life through his eyes. We pray for power to serve him better. To his bishop who had suggested a quiet time for the parish, a vicar exploded: "What my parish needs is not a quiet time, but an earthquake." We can sympathize with the impatience of the vicar, but true prayer does not confirm our complacency, it dispels it. It sends us out to serve in God's name those for whom we have prayed.

Here, then, are three simple exercises for the soul. Breathe in thoughts of God—of his greatness, his goodness, and his mercy. Lift up self and others to God in prayer. Reach out in love to someone in need. To do and repeat these exercises may not take long, but they can make the difference between a strong, joyous discipleship and a weak, unexercised, unused faith.

4.
The Thrust of Action

There is a sense in which we cannot be Christian alone. We must be Christian toward somebody. Often we experience God most truly when we forget ourselves and seek out those who need our help and friendship. Like the widow's cruse of oil, God often seems to renew our depleted energies. He continues to fill us with overflowing strength so long as there are the vessels of other lives into which we need to pour our love and service.

In Barre, Vermont, there is a famous granite quarry known as the "Rock of Ages." It is very deep. As one looks down from the observation platform, the workmen look small, indeed, as they cut away great blocks of granite from the sides and bottom of the pit.

One day some visitors were commenting on the depth of the quarry. "Yes," said one of the company officials, "but we have gone as deep as we can without going wider." When asked what he meant, he explained that the weight and pressure of the surrounding granite and earth are so great, that if the workers were to dig much deeper without making the quarry wider, there would be the danger of a cave-in.

Sometimes people set out in quest for God. Through meditation and prayer, they seek to deepen their sense of the reality of God's presence. But their quest, good as it is, is too self-centered. They are too concerned with achieving peace and joy for themselves, not enough with contributing these to others. Why does God fill our cup to overflowing if it is not so some of our faith and joy may flow out to others who are thirsty for understanding, justice, and love? This is what Ernest Crosby has tried to say in these lines:

> No one could tell me where my soul might be;
> I searched for God, and He eluded me;
> I sought my brother out, and found all three.[1]

Elton Trueblood began to challenge people, a few years ago, to take the yoke of Christ seriously by practicing certain disciplines in their lives. Many responded to this challenge and, by doing so, found their faith deepened and strengthened. After ten years, at Dr. Trueblood's invitation, some of the people met at Earlham College to evaluate the "yokefellow" emphasis. They decided that though it was good, it did not go far enough. What is needed now, the group decided, is to think of new ways by which Christian truth and love can be plowed out into the world of actual affairs. Christian ideals need to root themselves there in order to bring forth a new harvest of honesty, brotherhood, and justice in business, politics, international relations, and all the other activities of the world. Thus the plow was placed alongside the yoke as a necessary Christian symbol for our day, remembering that Jesus himself first used this symbol when he said, "No man, having put his hand to the plow, and looking back, is fit for the kingdom of God" (Luke 9:62).

This does not mean we should declare a moratorium on prayer. How can we do that and keep in vital touch with God? It does mean, however, that we should put a new emphasis on service and action. It is all too easy for churches in our day to turn concern for human suffering and need, and the problem of social ills, over to other agencies. The average church program is built largely around its own members. Some of this is necessary and important. However, there is much that a church can do to express its redemptive concern for the people of the community. Church members need a ministry that can help them to grow in faith and discipleship, and will root them even more deeply in the fellowship of the church. But sometimes church members need to forget themselves in service to others—service that reaches out into the community where spiritually people are dying for lack of attention, understanding, and love.

Why could not a church, for example, train its own Peace Corps groups to go out into the community in the name of the church to serve? We send church groups to foreign countries. Why not into our own communities? There could be groups to sponsor recreation for young people and for those who have passed the age of retirement. Christian caravans could help voters get to the polls on election day without, of course, telling them how to vote. If a church really thought that such demonstrations of Christian love were important, innumerable ways could be conceived to plow Christian love and concern out into the community and into the world in such a way that people would begin to get the idea that Christians are people who really care.

The church, of course, must not lose sight of its primary task which is much more than the temporary amelioration of social ills. Its task is to bring men and women into a vital relationship with God. It must, as Paul Tillich puts it, point to "something of ultimate significance, something which is independent of any change of fashion in thought and life." It must present what he calls "the healing power of the Christian message which is the power of reconciliation of the estranged and reunion of the separated." [2] This it can do only as it presents the love of God in Christ. But how are people going to understand this love on the vertical plane until they have seen love manifested among human beings? Even God had to stoop in love to our level before he could lift us up toward his. If it is true that one act of love speaks more loudly than many sermons, perhaps the church is missing a real opportunity to present Christ and his message through acts of love that reach out to people in their need regardless of who they are.

There may be those who think that the bulldozer is a better symbol of our age than the plow. Millions of children grow up in our towns and cities without ever seeing a plow in operation. They observe only bulldozers pushing back the debris of torn-down buildings, or pushing down trees, or scooping away precious topsoil to make room for new buildings or new roads. There are those today who would bulldoze us into conformity. There are even those who would coerce men in their religious affiliation. On a world front, we see communism trying to bulldoze its way into the rest of the world.

But the plow, not the bulldozer, has the last word. If the plow stops its work, the operator of the bulldozer cannot eat. Even in an atomic age, mankind is still dependent for its survival on the quiet, undramatic but ever mysterious sprouting of seeds. Far from being outmoded, the plow has become ultraimportant in our day as the problem of how to feed the rapidly expanding population of the world has become one of the greatest, if not the greatest, mankind has to solve.

Moreover, some things cannot be bulldozed into existence; they can only be cultivated and grown. Military might can force people into submission, but it cannot create true loyalty and love. Pressure tactics cannot bulldoze hate from people's hearts or force good will into them. Faith, hope, and love cannot be compelled. They can only grow from proper concepts planted in the hearts and minds of people. William Carey, the first modern missionary to India, stressed this truth in replying to Marquis Wellesley, brother of the Duke of Wellington and Governor-General of India. The Marquis asked, "Do you not think, Dr. Carey, it would be wrong to force the Hindoos to become Christians?" William Carey replied, "My Lord, the thing is impossible; we may indeed compel men to be hypocrites, but no power on earth can force men to become Christians." [3]

As a symbol of Christian progress and action, the plow is most appropriate. To do its work, *a plow must go beneath the surface* of the soil. If we are to get at the root causes of the world's troubles, we must get beneath the surface of man's sophistication and pride and ask some searching questions about the meaning of life and the nature of existence.

Why are we here? Where are we going? Are we merely animated atoms, or is the soul a reality? Is the goal of life "eat, drink, and be merry," or was Paul right when he said: "Whether therefore ye eat, or drink, or whatsoever ye do, do all to the glory of God" (1 Cor. 10:31)? Is death the final curtain of the play or only the end of the first act in an eternal drama? What makes us act as we do, and how can we be changed? Is the law of the state the highest law, or is there a higher? To whom or what do we owe our highest loyalty? Is man merely a puppet of the state, or is he a child of God? If he is a child of God, can the state do with him as it pleases, or must it respect his dignity as a person and his right to justice and to worship God?

These are not mere academic questions. They get at the root of man's moral and ethical behavior. The fate of millions in the world depends on how these questions are answered. They determine how people live in the world. Something in man seems to require that he believe in something other than himself—something spiritual and eternal. "If he renounces his soul," says Samuel H. Miller, "he drops below the brute world, as we tragically know from the horrible Nazi experiment. If he renounces God, as Russia does, he makes his politics a religion. He must make some guess as to the meaning of life and the purpose of history." [4]

If ever a person tried to go beneath the surface of things, that person was Paul, the apostle. He looked at the glittering cities of his day and saw their moral decay. He looked at corrupt leaders, so wise in the things of the world but such fools in ordering their own personal lives, or in knowing how to build a better society. He looked at human nature and saw the depths of depravity to which it could sink without God. He saw that no mere surface alteration would change this. Man needs to be changed down deep inside. He needs, said Paul, to become a new creature. Not just a creature of self-will as was Adam, not a creature of jealousy and hate as was Cain, but a creature of love—love that blossoms into obedience to the will of God; obedience that brings forth the fruit of the Spirit: "joy, peace, longsuffering, gentleness, goodness, faith, meekness, temperance" (Gal. 5:22–23).

Paul saw the impossibility of man making this change, becoming this new creature, without God's help. Looking at himself, he cried, "The good that I would I do not: but the evil which I would not, that I do. . . . For I delight in the law of God after the inward man: But I see another law in my members, warring against the law of my mind, and bringing me into captivity to the law of sin which is in my members" (Rom. 7:19, 22–23). No effort of will, no attempt to obey the law could solve this. Paul could keep the commandments against overt acts of evil and still be guilty inside of "all manner of concupiscence" (v. 8). Paul could not save himself. He had to be "rescued" from "the body of this death" (v. 24). Who could rescue him? Paul found the answer as he looked to the God he saw in Christ.

Paul saw the awful righteousness of God. "For the wrath of God is revealed from heaven against all ungodliness and unrighteousness of men" (Rom. 1:18). "Knowing therefore the terror of the Lord," he could say, "we persuade men" (2 Cor. 5:11). But Paul saw more. He saw the everlasting mercy. He saw "the light of the knowledge of the glory of God in the face of Jesus Christ" (2 Cor. 4:6). This was the answer—God's love revealed in Christ. Only this was big enough, strong enough, eternal enough to save man from himself and his sin. Knowing this, Paul could cry with joy, "I thank God through Jesus Christ our Lord" (Rom. 7:25).

Paul also saw man's desperate lack apart from an assurance of God's love and the hope of eternity. "If in this life only," he said, "we have hope in Christ, we are of all men most miserable" (1 Cor. 15:19). But in Christ and his resurrection, Paul saw the hope of mankind made real. "Now is Christ risen from the dead, and become the firstfruits of them that slept" (1 Cor. 15:20). Man's life is not to be seen just in the narrow limits of "threescore years and ten" but in the context of the eternity of God's love. In view of the hope revealed in Christ, Paul found the great incentive. "Therefore, my beloved brethren," he proclaimed, "be ye stedfast, unmoveable, always abounding in the work of the Lord, forasmuch as ye know that your labour is not in vain in the Lord" (1 Cor. 15:58).

Here, then, is the motive for Christian service. Life is seen as the handiwork of God. All personality, therefore, is to be respected as sacred. All men are to be seen as the object of God's love and concern. Life is to be considered in the light of its eternal destiny. In all this, God has shown that he is "able to make all grace abound" toward us that we "having all sufficiency in all things, may abound to every good work" (2 Cor. 9:8).

Again, the plow is an appropriate symbol of Christian progress and outreach, because if it is to do its work, *a plow must move forward*. If the church is to minister to its day, it must move forward in its efforts to make the Christian message relevant to the age in which it ministers. "Nothing," says Tillich, "could be more relevant for man than what concerns him ultimately." But the problem, he says, is how to present the new reality in Christ in such a way that people "who live in a largely secularized world can feel: This message concerns us ultimately; it is a matter of 'to be or not to be' for us." [5]

To do this, certainly the church needs to move forward in effective evangelism. But this is not a task for the clergy alone, nor must it be limited to the Sunday services of the church. This is the responsibility of the whole church, all the time. The workbench, because of a committed layman, can become a place where men feel the presence of the Carpenter of Nazareth. The office can become a place where a worker is known as one who is also engaged in the business of the King. The golf course can become a place where men can prove their discipleship to him who carried on so much of his ministry outdoors.

After all, Jesus did not do all his work in a synagogue. It was in a fisherman's boat that he challenged Simon to become a fisher of men. He bound Matthew to him, not at a church supper, but at a banquet of publicans. He changed a Samaritan woman's life as he showed her by the side of a well that God could be as real there, or in any other place, as in a temple on Mount Gerizim or Mount Zion. He went to the fisherman's boat because he wanted to catch Simon, not fish. He ate with "publicans and sinners" because "they that are whole need not a physician; but they that are sick" (Luke 5:31). Through his presence men felt a redemptive power working in their midst. Though many seem to have had no other desire than to be fed, others found the insight to say, "Lord, to whom shall we go? thou hast the words of eternal life" (John 6:68).

If laymen do not bear a living witness to their faith, there will be millions untouched by the Christian message. Many people never come under the sound of a preacher's voice until led to do so by the influence and invitation of some layman. Moreover, evangelism is not limited to the trained clergy. Every Christian by virtue of being a Christian is an evangelist in that he should want to share with others the faith that has brought new meaning and joy to his own life.

The church needs also to move forward in service to others. It is not true that the church has been idle in the face of human need. Every school which churches have built—and there have been thousands—every hospital, every mission station, every Christian center, every Christian home for children and for elderly people is an evidence of the church moving out in sacrificial love in response to human need. But there is more the churches can and must do. For example, not all suffering is physical. Much is caused by man's injustice to man. In Psalm 18 the author makes the interesting boast, "By my God have I leaped over a wall" (v. 29). There are walls in the world today over which millions of people cannot jump. These are social walls that begin in the minds of people, and when they are shared by enough people, they get projected out into life where they have vast social and moral consequences. Walls of prejudice and discrimination exist. Walls of nationalism and race have been erected. To those who cannot jump over them, they remain prison walls. What the church needs is some new Joshuas who will lead God's people to confront some of these walls, to walk around them until God's will concerning them becomes clear, and then to shout the truth that will make the walls of prejudice begin to crumble and fall. This we can do in the name of him who broke down the "middle wall of partition" (Eph. 2:14) between Jew and Gentile, and has made all one who will stand at the foot of the cross.

The church must always know in what direction to move in order to go forward. Otherwise, its efforts may not mean progress. Those who are experienced in plowing know how important it is, if one is to plow a straight furrow, to sight a distant object, such as a tree, a rock, or a fence post, and plow straight toward that.

"When a person becomes a Christian," Samuel H. Greene used to say, "he needs to study the Bible to learn the biblical basis of his faith." In a world of clashing ideologies, the Bible still stands supreme as a textbook for knowing God's will and purpose in history. There are those who think it is outmoded, but generation after generation comes back to its time-tested truths. The church must get back to the Bible if it wants to go forward. The Bible is a fixed star in the orbit of man's experience. It directs man's attention to the unchanging righteousness and love of God, shining through the law and the prophets, and shining with perfect luminosity through the person and work of Jesus Christ.

Clarence Darrow, famous criminal lawyer of a few years ago, once remarked to Dr. Joseph Sizoo, "Life is an unpleasant interruption of nothingness." In other words, we came from nothing, we return to nothing, and life between is only an unpleasant interlude. With all the splendid equipment with which he had to work—a brilliant mind, a genuine concern for the underdog, an international reputation—because he believed in no ultimate purpose, no Supreme Being, his furrow veered off in the direction of bitter cynicism. One is reminded of Mephistopheles' remark to Faust, "The sum total of everything is nothing." In a world where there is much to indicate the goodness of God, those who hold this philosophy veer off in the direction of futility and despair.

Paul knew much that could have tempted him to despair. In spite of his brilliant mind and his sense of mission, he had a "thorn in the flesh" and experienced persecution as few men have had to suffer it. But Paul believed there was an eternal landmark. "I determined," he said, "not to know any thing among you, save Jesus Christ, and him crucified" (1 Cor. 2:2). Again he said, "This one thing I do, forgetting those things which are behind, and reaching forth unto those things which are before, I press toward the mark for the prize of the high calling of God in Christ Jesus" (Phil. 3:13–14). Once again, he said, "For to me to live is Christ" (Phil. 1:21). This was his landmark. Look at his furrow of hope stretching straight into eternity itself: "and to die is gain." Even death, he believed, would not stop or change the direction of his furrow as it led straight to the heart of God.

Finally, the plow is an appropriate symbol of Christian progress and outreach, for if a plow is to do its work, *there must be some power to pull it.*

This is a world that knows a lot about power. There is water power, candle power, horsepower, electric power, and now atomic power. Man now has enough power to shoot men and objects into outer space and to blast life off the face of the globe. Man is both blessed and cursed by the power he has learned to use.

Not all power, however, is in the hands of the scientist and engineer. There is spiritual power without which life could never be transformed. There is the power to change a sinful youth into a St. Augustine. Power exists to create the witness of the Christian faith and to keep it strong in history in spite of the weaknesses of the churches. There is the power to change human lives and to start them on an upward trail, endowing them with new hope and purpose. There is power, as the author of Revelation puts it, to "make all things new" (21:5).

Halford Luccock used to tell about a student who disdainfully dismissed religion as a "lot of moonshine." To the student's surprise, Luccock agreed with him. He asked the student if he had ever watched the tides come in, and if he knew what caused them to do so. The answer, suggested Luccock, is "moonshine." For tides are caused by the pull of the moon on the earth—the pull of another world on this. And that, said Luccock, is what religion is. It is the pull of the world of the Spirit on the world of the flesh.

Why do we keep on striving for a better world in terms of high ideals? Why don't we just give up and settle for a world of sin, violence, and hate? Something won't let us give up; something keeps pulling us on; something makes us know that these things are evil and wrong. Psychologists now confirm what theologians long have said—that a deep-seated sense of guilt lies at the bottom of much of the neuroses of our day. Something won't let us break the moral laws with impunity. The psychologist, Ernest Ligon, says,

Whether a personal God exists or not, it makes a tremendous difference to a man's mental health as to whether or not he has faith in a personal God. To have the deepest confidence that there is a God, who does hear and answer one's prayer, forms a basis for courage which makes a man able to meet many of life's severest trials with mental poise. On the other hand, to hold the belief that this is a purely mechanical universe, which has no heart and is utterly unfriendly, has led many a man to a suicide of hopelessness.[6]

Why? Men pray in times of crisis because they cannot help it. Why? Without some kind of a faith in God, man is lonely even in the midst of a crowded world. Why? As Augustine put it, "Thou madest us for thyself, and we can find no rest till we find rest in thee." The enemies of Jesus won their point. They succeeded in having Jesus crucified. But history has reversed the verdict as to who really won that day. Why? Something seems to be pulling on history; something will not let us go on pretending wrong is right.

That something—that power that causes the seeds to sprout and pulls the tides along—can take a simple life of faith and use it to lift life to a higher level, just as a cross was taken and used to lift men out of their sins. For this is the amazing truth. We can be channels of that power. Not like a wooden trough through which water flows unable to partake of the wood over which it goes, but more like a mind that is captivated by a great idea and is moved to live in terms of it. Men cannot bring in the kingdom of God by their own efforts. They are neither wise enough nor good enough. Men themselves must be changed by God's power, a power that can help them to overcome lust and hate. Men must permit themselves to be pulled in the direction in which God wants them to go.

"No man, having put his hand to the plow"—a plow that digs beneath the earth's surface, a plow that to do its work must move forward, a plow that must submit to a pulling power—what a symbol for our day as we seek to solve the problems of our world, and as we move in the direction of fulfilling a greater measure of God's will.

5. The Importance of Following Through

In his translation of the Bible, James Moffatt brings out clearly the meaning of Paul's statement in Philippians 1:6. It reads, "Of this I am confident, that he who has begun the good work in you, *will go on completing it* until the day of Jesus Christ." God always follows through. The Shepherd of souls will not leave his sheep stranded in the desert. If they will follow him, he will lead them all the way to the fold.

We are not always as certain to follow through. It is so easy for us to go part of the way and then quit. In fact, it was this tendency on the part of halfhearted disciples that caused Jesus to utter his statement about the plow. It was not the plow Jesus had in mind, much as it can be used as a symbol of Christian thrust into the community and the world, but the plower. Unless the plower follows through, the plow cannot do its work.

A good farmer looks ahead of him as he plows and keeps at the task until it is finished. That is why Jesus' statement is so effective: "No man, having put his hand to the plow, *and looking back,* is fit for the kingdom of God" (Luke 9:62). Yet this is the danger in Christian discipleship as, indeed, in almost every other area of life—the danger of failing to follow through. It is so much easier to start a thing than it is to finish it. It is the ability to keep on going that often tests our fortitude and spells the difference between success and failure in our efforts.

"Perhaps the most difficult problem in the psychology of motivation," writes Ernest Ligon, "is that of sustained effort." [1] How to keep on keeping on—that is our problem. It is so much easier to stop halfway, to get tired and quit, to lose interest and enthusiasm, to peter out.

This is the real problem in the practice of prayer. If we have been neglecting our devotional life, we may make up our mind to start reading the Bible and to spend some time in prayer every day. We intend to follow through. But we get busy doing other things—or we get tired—or we lack the necessary will power. After a while, like so many times before, we fall back into neglect and loss of interest. Or we decide to give up a habit—and the same thing happens. We are not like satellites orbiting through outer space with little or no resistance to overcome. We are subject to all the gravitational pull of human nature. Unless we have the thrust of a great experience, a great faith, a great commitment, we are apt to be slowed down in our efforts to live the good life and in our venture in discipleship with Christ.

Without the quality of "stick-to-it-iveness," many a person, even though he possessed the quality of genius, would have been a failure. William Carey showed genius in three fields. He was a great and gifted missionary. He was also brilliant as a philologist and translator. Had he failed to pursue these areas, William Carey would still have been known as a great botanist. But he did not credit any success that he may have had to genius. To his nephew, Eustace, he once said, "If after my removal, any one should think it worth his while to write my life, I will give you a criterion by which you may judge its correctness. If he give me credit for being a plodder, he will describe me justly. Any thing beyond this will be too much. I can plod. I can persevere in any definite pursuit. To this I owe every thing." [2]

His life bears this out. It was in 1787 that he proposed to a group of ministers a discussion of the question, "Have the churches of Christ done all they ought to have done for heathen nations?" He was met by a strong rebuff from the extreme Calvinist, John Ryland, who said, "Young man, sit down; when God pleases to convert the heathen world, he will do it without your help or mine either." [3] But five years later, in his famous sermon on Isaiah 44:2–3 preached at a meeting of churches in Nottingham, England, he was still pursuing his great missionary idea under the headings: "Expect Great Things from God," and "Dare Great Things for God." When it looked as if the session was going to take no action on his suggestions, he said, "Are you, after all, going again to do nothing?" This time he got results, for the meeting passed a resolution calling for the formation of a "Baptist Society for propagating the Gospel among the Heathen." [4]

Carey himself became the first missionary. He labored many years for his first convert. Turning his gift for languages to good use, he translated the Bible into the Bengali language. Carey met strong opposition from government sources. "But you know, sir," the Governor-General complained, "that the Bible tells us that all men are on a level; now it will never do to circulate that in this country. If the natives get the idea that they are equal to us, farewell to the British government in India." [5] But William Carey had a great idea and a great sense of mission. And he could plod. The result is that the story and the work of his life constitutes one of the great chapters in the history of the Christian church.

The same quality of determination to see a thing through characterized the inventive genius of Thomas Edison. To conceive a thing may take brilliance. To carry it out takes work. Edison was capable of both. It was his genius that suggested a possible way to produce light by electricity. The almost unanimous opinion of scientists was that it could not be done, since it would be necessary to subdivide electricity. That, they argued, would be contrary to the law of conservation of energy. Edison, however, believed it could be done. His biographer, Mary Childs Nerney, tells us that having conceived the idea, he first set himself to the task of reading "everything in print on gas which then dominated the illuminating field." She goes on to say, "He devoured journals and proceedings of scientific societies until, when he had finished, he knew more about gas than experts in the field." [6]

As was his custom, Edison wrote down his goal in one of his famous black notebooks: "Object: Edison to effect exact imitation of all done by gas, so as to replace lighting by gas by lighting by electricity." He then began to search for something of high resistance that could be used in small diameter as a filament (he coined the word) so as to produce incandescent light. Carbon has high resistance to electricity, so after working steadily for thirty-six hours, Edison managed to carbonize a piece of cotton thread and place it in a glass bulb from which he then drew some of the air. When the electric current was applied, the thread produced a steady light—for forty hours—until Edison increased the current and burned it out.

The idea had been proved possible, but the work of achieving an electric light had just begun. Carbonized thread was too fragile. He thought platinum might work, but it was too scarce and expensive. Perhaps a fiber would work. Edison spent ten years experimenting with over six thousand specimens of fiber from all over the world before he finally discovered that a manufactured cellulose, and later tungsten, would work. Many urged him to quit. It is said that after testing seven hundred fibers, none of which proved successful, one of his colleagues advised him to give up the quest since they had not found out a thing. Edison replied, "We have found out one thing very important. We have found seven hundred things that don't work." It is to his perseverance as well as to his genius that we are indebted. He stayed at the task until he found something that would work to produce electric light.

How does one get the ability to follow through? Obviously, will power is part of the answer. It takes will power to carry out any resolution, whether it is to diet, to save, to begin a new prayer life, to give up an old habit, to begin a new one, or to do anything that calls for discipline and effort. It often requires real strength of character to say, "I will" or "I won't." As John Drinkwater says in his poem, "Purpose"—"But, Lord, the will—there lies our bitter need."

In order to succeed, however, the will needs help. If it fights alone, it often loses the battle. For will power to be effective, one's whole self must be engaged in the battle. One must be convinced that the thing for which he strives is important—that it is more important than the habits, practices, indolence it is meant to replace or overcome. The person who says he is too busy to go to church just doesn't think it is important enough for him to make the effort to go. If he did, he would find the time to go.

Indeed, Guy Bowden[7] argues that often we are unable to give up a sin or bad habit, not because the will is weak, but because it is too strong; not because it doesn't function, but because it functions all too well. It supports us in the thing we really want—in what we really think is important and necessary to our happiness. We may tell our mind one thing, but down deep never completely release whatever it is we want to overcome. We never completely accept the fact that we can get along without it. We never convince our imagination that we mean business, never completely renounce what we say we want to give up.

We are like Augustine who in his early years prayed, "Lord, give me chastity, but not yet." Or we are like Demas who forsook Paul and the Christian cause, "having loved this present world" (2 Tim. 4:10). We want God, but we also want to love this present world, and often the world wins out. Or we may lack the experience to know how pleasurable a new course of action may be. We need encouragement. We need a stimulus. That is why J. A. Hadfield says that "what the will requires for

its strength and development is not training but inspiration." [8]
When we want something badly enough, when we really think
it is important to our happiness, if it is within reason, we can
usually find a way to accomplish it.

That is why incentive is so important. Someone has said that
the word "incentive" is the biggest word in the English language. That may be so. Certainly, little is accomplished without
it. A mother may scold her son until she is blue in the face to
get him to shine his shoes but without much success. Then one
day her son meets an attractive girl, and he begins to shine his
shoes without being told to do so. Junior has met an incentive.
A person would not voluntarily enter a burning building, but if
his child is in there, he will risk his life to enter it. The desire
to rescue his child provides the individual with a stronger incentive than do the natural instincts of fear and self-preserva-
tion.

As an incentive to a more satisfying prayer life and a deepened Christian experience, many are turning to participation
in small groups. These people through fellowship, Bible study,
and prayer help each other to lay hold more firmly on the
deeper things of spiritual life. The bishops of the Church of
England have become so convinced of the value of such groups
within the church, that they said in a recent report, "Without
such inner groups the work of present-day evangelism cannot
go forward." The effectiveness of such groups is described by
John L. Casteel. By personal groups he means "a small number
of persons, meeting face to face regularly for the purposes of
the study of the Bible and of the Christian faith; for prayer;
for the exchange of experiences, needs, and insights; and for
taking thought as to how they can best fulfil their calling as
Christians to love and serve God and other people." [9] When
people join together for such a purpose, he says, "they often
discover an increment of power among them that seems to be
something beyond the simple addition of their numbers. They

stimulate one another's minds, stir up energies, encourage wills." [10]

A person wanting to deepen his prayer life, or strengthen his Christian discipleship, could do no better than to get together a few like-minded friends. With them begin on some regular basis to meet together for prayer and Bible study and perhaps the study of some outstanding book of devotional literature. It might be well to study such a book as John Casteel's for suggestions and guidance as how best to proceed. In the process, new incentive may be gained and Christ's promise claimed: "Where two or three are gathered together in my name, there am I in the midst of them" (Matt. 18:20).

Our faith in God through Christ, of course, provides our greatest incentive for the living of the Christian life, just as the life of Jesus remains our perfect example of how it should be done. For Jesus, the desire to do the will of God was the supreme motivation of his life. He, too, was tempted to turn aside. When the Greeks came seeking him he said: "Now is my soul troubled; and what shall I say? Father, save me from this hour: but," he continued, "for this cause came I unto this hour. [I will say] Father, glorify thy name" (John 12:27-28). His sense of mission was a stronger incentive than his desire to turn aside. He feared to hurt his Father more than he feared death on a cross.

When a Christian comes to the place where he finds real joy in serving the Lord, where the approval of the Lord becomes more important and satisfying than any acts of indifference or sin he may be tempted to embrace, he has found the secret of following through in his Christian life. Indeed, if he can be tempted to turn aside, as someone has pointed out, he is partly willing. He needs an experience that will put God supremely at the center of his desire.

As one travels from Worcester to Boston, if he is listening to his car radio, an interesting thing happens. As one leaves

Worcester, he may be listening to a broadcast from station WTAG. But in a few miles, as he proceeds east on Route 9, another station begins to come in. If he continues on his way to Boston and does not change his radio dial, soon the Worcester broadcast fades out. He will then hear only the program of station WEEI in Boston.

So it is when one draws near to God in prayer, in Christian worship, and in fellowship. When one associates with Christian friends, the signals of the world get weaker, and the message of Christian faith and discipleship becomes stronger and clearer. It begins to fill one's heart with joy. Thomas Chalmers, in a famous sermon, called this "The Expulsive Power of a New Affection." "What can not be thus destroyed," he said, "may be dispossessed—and one taste may be made to give way to another, and to lose its power entirely as the reigning affection of the mind." [11]

This is not easy, and often it takes a crisis experience to bring it about. God sometimes has to break our heart in order to get our full attention. At least he has to humble it and make it contrite. This he can do if we will keep him tuned in, for he is always broadcasting his love from the cross.

It is not enough, as Guy Bowden says, to tell a person to repent. He may not know how. It is not enough to tell him to say his prayers. He needs more help than that. But if he can see Christ on a cross and realize that his sins helped to put him there, unless he has a heart of stone, it will begin to melt. He will turn to God in deeper penitence and faith. It is that constant vision, supported by the worship and fellowship of the church, that begets love in return. It makes prayer a desire, not a duty, and helps mind, heart, and will to pull together in the same direction as a team. Even then it may sometimes take all the strength of will a person has to keep from turning the dial away from God before the message of his love has had a chance to come in strong and clear.

This is why we need the help and encouragement of others of like human nature as ourselves, who have persevered in the faith, and give evidence of real joy in Christian discipleship. This is why we need the church. To think that all alone we can become the kind of a Christian God wants us to be is to be guilty of what Elton Trueblood calls "the angelic fallacy." We could if we were angels. But we are not angels. We are weak, human beings. We are what Paul called "earthen vessels" (2 Cor. 4:7). We need all the pull God can exert on our lives, plus all the push we can get from the influence, the example, the love, and sympathetic encouragement of others who seem to be standing strong and true in the faith.

The perfect example of one who followed through is Jesus. Even as a child he set out to be about his Father's business. Later in life, temptations sought to deter him. The crowds sought to turn his head by demanding that he become their king. The disciples misunderstood him and feared for his safety. "Master," they once said, "the Jews of late sought to stone thee; and goest thou thither again?" (John 11:8). The leaders sought to destroy him. The awful prospect of the cross loomed ahead. But having put his hand to the plow, he never looked back. His furrow runs straight through Gethsemane to Calvary. "Having loved his own . . . he loved them unto the end" (John 13:1). He remained "obedient unto death, even the death of the cross" (Phil. 2:8). And at last he could say, "It is finished" (John 19:30). Not just his life was finished. His mission was accomplished. By his life he had revealed perfect obedience to the will of God, even to the acceptance of the cross.

None of us will be able to say at death that his work on earth is completely finished. There is so much we have failed to do that we should have done, but we can keep plowing in the right direction. Having put our hand to the plow, we can pray for dedication to follow through. Some years ago, James H.

Franklin remarked, "The kingdom of God is out ahead. We may not enter it in our generation, but please God when we fall, let us fall with our faces toward it."

We have considered the symbol of the plow as we seek to translate Christian commitment into terms of world service. We have thought of the power necessary to pull it. Now we have considered the role of the plower. Life is often a long, hard pull. We are weak. We get tired so soon. The temptation often comes to quit or turn aside. We must pray with Sir Francis Drake, "O God when Thou givest to Thy servants to endeavour any great matter, make them also to know that it is not the beginning but the continuing of the same until it be thoroughly finished, which yieldeth the true glory, through Him that for the finishing of Thy work laid down His life, even Jesus Christ our Lord. Amen." [12]

6.
The Call to
Witness

The best way to keep the cup of faith overflowing is to offer its contents to other lips. Christian faith is given to be shared, not hoarded. Like the widow's cruse of oil, the more one's faith is poured out in love and witness, the more it is replenished. In fact, Jesus relies on such sharing for the building of his kingdom on earth. "He draws one man to him," says Charles E. Jefferson, "infuses into him a new spirit, sends him after one brother man, who in time goes after a third man, and this third man after a fourth, and thus does he weld a chain by means of which Caesar shall be dragged from his throne." [1]

To know Jesus was to want to tell others about him. John the Baptist told his disciples. Andrew told his brother, Simon. Philip told Nathanael. The woman of Samaria told a whole village. "Come, see a man," she said, "which told me all things that ever I did: is not this the Christ? . . . many of the Samaritans of that city," we are told, "believed on him for the saying of the woman" (John 4:29,39).

This is the natural sequence of a true Christian experience: first the experience, then the witness; first the joy of knowing, then the joy of telling; first the experience of grace, then the expression of gladness; first the miracle of mercy—"God was in Christ, reconciling the world unto himself," then the mission —"and hath committed unto us the word of reconciliation" (2 Cor. 5:19).

Paul would remind us that we have this treasure in "earthen vessels" (2 Cor. 4:7). It is the contents, not the cup, of which we boast. "We preach not ourselves," said Paul, "but Christ Jesus the Lord" (2 Cor. 4:5). What Jesus said to the Gadarene is still our best guidance—"shew how great things God hath done unto thee" (Luke 8:39).

The Bible repeatedly stresses the importance of sharing our faith. "Let the redeemed of the Lord say so," urges the psalmist (107:2). The author of Proverbs writes, "He that winneth souls is wise" (11:30). In a similar vein, the author of Daniel says, "They that be wise shall shine as the brightness of the firmament; and they that turn many to righteousness as the stars for ever and ever" (12:3).

In fact, the entire Bible is a book of evangelism. That is, its purpose is to convert, not just to instruct; to evangelize, not just to educate. It calls for decision and commitment. "I have set before you life and death," cried Moses, "therefore choose life, that both thou and thy seed shall live" (Deut. 30:19). "Choose you this day whom ye will serve," said Joshua (24:15). John says of his writings, "These are written, that ye might believe that Jesus is the Christ, the Son of God; and that believing ye might have life through his name" (20:31). And Jesus said, "The harvest truly is great, but the labourers are few: pray ye therefore the Lord of the harvest, that he would send forth labourers into his harvest" (Luke 10:2).

Jesus began early to train his followers in the art of witnessing to their faith. In a program of outreach that we might call "Operation Seventy," he "appointed other seventy also, and sent them two and two before his face into every city and place, whither he himself would come" (Luke 10:1). By this means, he not only prepared the way for his own ministry in these places but provided his followers with actual clinical experience in meeting the problems and experiencing the rewards and disappointments of personal witnessing. It was not an easy assignment on which he was sending them. "Behold," he warned, "I send you forth as lambs among wolves" (v. 3).

They were to rely wholly on the hospitality of those to whom they were sent. "Carry neither purse, nor scrip, nor shoes," Jesus instructed them (v. 4). To submit to such radical self-denial would both test their faith and affirm their sincerity. They were to hasten to declare their message. They were to heal the sick and declare the nearness of God and his kingdom to the people.

One can imagine the timidity with which many of them set out on such a new venture. Surely it was to give them added courage and confidence that Jesus sent them out in pairs. Rebuffs they must have met. It must have been difficult, even in a land where hospitality is proverbial, to depend so completely on the goodness of the people for food and lodging. But Luke tells us they returned "with joy" (10:17). Then Jesus asked them, "When I sent you without purse, and scrip, and shoes, lacked ye any thing?" They replied, "Nothing" (22:35). Lack anything. On the contrary, they declared, "Even the devils are subject unto us through thy name" (10:17). Whatever they lacked in material advantages was more than made up by the surge of new spiritual power which they experienced as they gave witness to their newfound faith.

But how does one witness to his faith? This is our problem. How can we effectively communicate our faith to an indifferent and cynical world? The answer to this question is important both for the sake of the world and for our faith. A faith unshared will, in time, become a faith unknown.

The individual who would have his faith overflow in a loving witness to others must first of all have a genuine love for people. He must pray to love people as Jesus loved them. Jesus did not love people in order to manipulate them. In fact, he decried the exploitation motive in human relationships. "Ye know that they which are accounted to rule over the Gentiles exercise lordship over them; and their great ones exercise authority upon them. But so shall it not be among you" (Mark 10:42–43), he said. Jesus emphasized, instead, the service motive. "Whosoever will be great among you, shall be your minister: And whosoever of you will be the chiefest, shall be servant of all" (Mark 10:43–44).

Even our enemies, Jesus said, should come within the scope of our love. This does not mean that we will like everyone we meet. It does mean we must try to exercise Christian love toward them. And this, said Jesus, means at least three things. It means we must try to bless them, do good to them, and pray for them. "Bless them that curse you," he said, "do good to them that hate you, and pray for them which despitefully use you, and persecute you" (Matt. 5:44). If it is our purpose to bless those people with whom we come in contact, opportunities for sharing our faith will often open up to us.

In asking how our faith can overflow in radiant witness, one answer is quite obvious. One declares his faith by living it. Words carry little weight unless they are backed up by performance. "I'd rather see a sermon than hear one any day," wrote Edgar Guest. While this can easily be made an excuse for neglecting public worship, it does stress the need of joining faith to deed. "Those things, which ye have both learned, and received, and heard, *and seen in me*, do," Paul could write to the Philippian Christians (4:9). Jesus contrasted word and deed when he spoke of the father who said to his sons (Matt. 21:28–30), "Son, go work to day in my vineyard." The first son said, "I will not," but he "repented, and went." The second son said, "I go, sir," but he "went not." It is quite obvious which son was the more loyal to his father.

Example alone, however, is not enough. Sometimes there must be a spoken witness. When an insurance salesman who was a close friend to Henry Ford learned that the great inventor had purchased a large insurance policy through an agent whom he hardly knew, the friend asked, "Why didn't you buy it from me?" Mr. Ford's answer was brief but revealing—"You never asked me," he replied. Thousands are outside the Christian fold today because those on the inside have never asked them to come in.

Many are extremely reluctant to speak to others on matters of Christian faith. They feel timid—timid perhaps because of inexperience in speaking about the deep things of the soul. We do not ask another how he gets along with his wife. Why, some would contend, should we ask him about his personal relationship to God? We do not advertise our deepest feelings to the world. Sometimes we have difficulty expressing them to the ones we love best. Likewise, many individuals hesitate to express to another who may not understand, or even care, their deepest thoughts about God. Often we feel unworthy to speak about our faith because we know that our lives have been such poor reflections of it. We fear we may sound condescending, or even hypocritical, if we claim to possess what another needs.

Some are reluctant to speak of their faith because they think science has put religion on the defensive. Science, they say, talks about what it can prove; religion they falsely define as "something you believe but can't prove." But the most important things of life—the very things that make life most worth living—are precisely the things that cannot be proved by scientific weight or measurement. Who can prove God by laboratory methods? The heart, not the test tube, is the place God must be found. We find him in the laboratory of experience, not the laboratory of scientific experiment. We cannot prove him. We can only live by faith in him and let him prove himself. Or we can discard faith in him and see what happens. For without faith in God, we become adrift on life's baffling sea with no dependable star to guide us. Life becomes a cheaper thing. Standards become untrustworthy. There is no ultimate standard by which to judge right from wrong. Human judgment warped by prejudice and pride becomes our only yardstick by which to measure our actions. Immortality becomes a vain hope. Without faith in God, life becomes a vain struggle to find meaning in a meaningless world.

Some hesitate to speak about their faith because they want to appear as men of the world, liberated from the confining restrictions of religion. Granted that religion has often been presented mostly as a mass of restrictions; yet when we liberate ourselves from our Christian faith and heritage, we release ourselves from the very roots that have given us the finest fruits of our civilization. This is why Elton Trueblood calls ours a "cut-flower" civilization. A flower cut from its roots is free—free to die. Life cut from its roots in God is free to live without a comforting presence in time of sorrow, a source of forgiveness in time of guilt, and a sustaining hope in the face of death.

Some are reluctant to speak to others about religious faith because they think of it as an intrusion into another's private life. A college professor was invited to preach in a nearby church. When he returned to the campus, a student asked him, "Did you convert anyone?" The professor replied, "I was too much of a gentleman to ask."

But is a person more of a gentleman because he refrains from asking about the most important relationship in the world? If God and immortality are true, then faith in God is the most important thing in the world. We ask another person about his golf score, his physical condition, his business success. Why should we not ask about that which can give his life its highest purpose, can turn his household into a Christian home, and can give him an eternal hope?

Is the doctor any less of a gentleman because he asks his patient about his symptoms? Is the stewardess less of a person because she asks, "Is your seat belt fastened?" It is not morbid curiosity that prompts such questions but a genuine concern for another's welfare. The insurance agent does not think it awkward to ask a prospective client if he needs more insurance. It is a strange world where it is considered proper to ask a person if he has enough insurance, but not whether he has the assurance of eternal life.

If we think that evangelism and personal witnessing are antiquated, certainly the Communists do not think so. They believe in telling their message loud and long. They exalt Lenin as their Messiah and the Communist party as their god. Party members are thoroughly indoctrinated. They are expected to witness to their doctrines and the Communist way of life. True, their performance reveals a strange conception of the meaning of such words as justice, democracy, and peace. They do not, however, depend on the mere osmosis of influence to extend their faith and cause. They literally shout their message from the street corners as loud speakers blare forth their twisted version of history. We cannot hope to match this kind of aggressive evangelism with a weak, apologetic approach to our faith.

Of course, the person who wants to let his faith overflow, in a way that will bring a blessing to others, has the church as a channel through which he may express his beliefs. By the very act of being affiliated with a Christian church, one publicly declares his Christian faith to others. The man who walks with his family up the steps of his church is declaring to all who see that he is glad to be known as one who loves the Lord.

How to go beyond this is our problem. It is to people in the everyday world that we must learn to communicate our faith if God is to become vital in the affairs of men. Not just the pulpit but the office, not just the quiet time but the coffee break, not just the prayer tower but the place of recreation, not just the Lord's table but the conference table and the dinner table, not just the altar but the laboratory—these must become places where God is recognized and honored. This is where we most need to know how to communicate our faith. We must make our beliefs known in a winsome and compelling way if faith in God is to be an effective force in our world.

Philip, one of the disciples, gives a good example of an overflowing faith. While traveling south from Jerusalem to Gaza, he was overtaken by an Ethiopian official reading in his chariot. "Then the Spirit," Luke tells us, "said unto Philip, Go near, and join thyself to the chariot" (Acts 8:29). This was the first step if Philip was to bear his witness. He must go where the person was. He could not wait until the stranger got out of his chariot and came to him. He must go to the stranger.

Here is where the church today faces its greatest problem. How can it carry its message to the vast multitudes of people who never darken the doors of a church? To do so, the church must depend more upon its laymen. Professional religious leaders can do their part. Efforts have been made with some success to establish industrial chaplains who can minister to workers in factories. Military chaplains carry the gospel to men in the armed services. Even here, much of their effectiveness is in dealing with men who seldom, if ever, attend the services of the chapel. It is the individual layman, however, speaking in face-to-face contacts that can do the most good. People expect a clergyman to speak of religion. They reason that this is what he is paid to do. The layman has nothing to gain except the satisfaction of sharing with another a faith that has meant much to him.

Moreover, the layman has this advantage—he is already where the other person is. He is already at the shop, in the office, in the laboratory. He already has the confidence and acceptance of his fellow workers. If he can conceive of his vocation as a channel of service to God as well as man, he can make it a daily witness to Christian faith and conduct. He can hold himself ready, as opportunity presents itself, to speak about his faith.

Again, if one wants his faith to overflow in loving witness, he must use tact in his approach to another person. Philip did not begin by telling the Ethiopian something but by asking him something. "Understandest thou what thou readest?" (Acts 8:30). He did not impose himself upon the stranger, but waited to be invited by showing a friendly interest in him.

A bridge of confidence and acceptance must be built. Friendship and love, a genuine interest in another's problems—these are still the keys that unlock another's heart. Life leaves all of us with many unanswered questions. Most of all, we want to know the meaning of life. If a person can help others to ask these questions and can show how he found an answer that gives peace and hope in the face of life's trials and uncertainties, he is in a position to help others find a more satisfying answer to their own deepest needs.

Admittedly, in the Ethiopian's case, this was relatively easy. He was already interested in religion. He was reading the Jewish Scriptures. But he was reading without understanding. He needed help, and when help was tactfully offered, he gladly accepted it.

Not everyone is so eager to hear about religion. Often spiritual hunger is buried deep beneath thick layers of indifference, and even antagonism, caused by past hurts, neglect, material success, or sheer sinful indulgence. Sometimes it is caused by a false concept of religion. Whatever the reasons, much of modern life is out of touch with God.

Yet, the hunger is there. Men may not recognize it. They may not admit that it exists. But they are looking for something that can give them a sense of true fulfilment in their lives. They may seek this in strange places. It is not easy to understand much that modern art, literature, and music are trying to say to us. Some of it is a brave, even brash, attempt to break out of the traditional and explore new realms of thought and expression. Much of it, however, reveals the hollow meaninglessness of our age. The modern artist, novelist, and musician are crying out against life as it often seems today. They know what they are crying against, but do not know the answer.

Philip had an answer. Indeed, for him, it was *the* answer. He began at the point of the man's interest and "preached unto him Jesus" (Acts 8:35). This is where an overflowing Christian witness really begins—in the conviction that Christ is the answer to our deepest needs. Undoubtedly, Philip told about his experiences with Jesus—how Jesus had called him, and how he had followed. We know that he talked about the cross, for he began with the passage in Isaiah that the Ethiopian was reading, and by which he was puzzled: "He was led as a sheep to the slaughter; and like a lamb dumb before his shearer, so opened he not his mouth" (v. 32). No doubt Philip pointed out how this Scripture passage was fulfilled in the life and death of Jesus. We can be sure he talked about the resurrection, for he spoke of baptism by which the resurrection is symbolized. He must have gone on to tell how the disciples were going everywhere telling the story of what God had done, and is doing, through Christ. He probably pointed out that those who responded in faith to their message were being baptized.

Of course, Philip had the advantage of having known Jesus. When he talked about the cross and the resurrection, he was talking about matters of which he had firsthand knowledge. The layman, too, must speak about that of which he has had firsthand experience. Being theologically untrained, the average person may be hesitant to speak of the theological aspects of Jesus' life and death. He can, however, share what the Christian fellowship means to him and to his family. The layman can tell what the Christian faith has meant to him in times of trouble and deep sorrow. He can discuss what he thinks it means to follow Christ in one's personal, family, business, and social life.

Philip did not begin with the church. Important as it is, the church does not come first. Eventually Philip must have spoken about the church and its symbols, for the Ethiopian requested baptism. But Philip did not begin there. He began with Jesus. Many people are outside the Christian churches today because they are critical of what happens, or fails to happen, within the churches. They cannot, however, so easily dismiss the Saviour. He is the answer to our deepest questions.

The Christian who can tell in his own words how Christ has proved to be the answer in his own life has something worthwhile to share with his neighbor.

Fortunately, Philip knew his Scriptures. He recognized at once the passage in Isaiah from which the Ethiopian was reading. Therefore, in conversing with the Ethiopian, he could begin "at the same scripture" (Acts 8:35). Where better could he have begun to interpret Jesus? To be a Communist, one must know the writings of Marx and Lenin. To be an effective Christian, one should know the Bible. Somewhere in the Bible there is a starting point for every human situation. Fortunate is the person who knows where to turn to find the Bible passage that most speaks to his situation.

But Philip knew more. He knew Jesus. He knew the cross. He knew that in no other life, and in no other event, is Isaiah's prophetic insight so clearly revealed. Here was one who gave himself in utter obedience, utter love, utter self-denial to do the will of God. It was not just Pilate who put Jesus on the cross. God put him there. God who guided Jesus' every thought and act was in that supreme event, suffering for the sins of the world.

When the Ethiopian was able to see Christ as God's answer to his need, and the Christian faith as the answer to his quest, Philip led him to the point of personal commitment. His commitment was sealed with the act of baptism. This the church is able to do as it gives the believer a channel through which to experience Christian commitment, fellowship, outreach, and growth. With new faith and assurance in his heart, the traveler in Gaza who had journeyed far to seek an answer to his spiritual quest went "on his way rejoicing" (Acts 8:39).

The world today is dying for lack of love—for lack of a dynamic, transforming, challenging faith. It is looking for those who claim to know the answer. We can begin right where we are by sharing the Christian answer. If we can help another person to believe that we have a better answer, and if he sees that the Christian answer has made a difference in us, we will have fulfilled a real purpose before we, like Philip, are "caught away." We have the message. How to say it in relevant terms is our problem. The message remains, "Come, see a man, which told me all things that ever I did: is not this the Christ?" (John 4:29).

7. The Source of Spiritual Power

Discipline, spiritual exercises, outgoing love and service, follow-through, witnessing—these are all important aids to spiritual growth and power. This does not mean, however, that we can create our own spiritual power. All the spiritual exercises in the world will not produce spiritual power, unless they lead us to a deeper faith in God who hears and answers prayer. "He that cometh to God," says the author of Hebrews, "must believe that he is, and that he is a rewarder of them that diligently seek him" (11:6).

One can no more create faith and spiritual power by his own efforts than a flower can make itself grow. The flower grows in response to soil, sun, and rain. So it is with faith. Faith is a response, not an achievement. Christian faith is a response to God's redemptive love in Christ. The trouble with so many people is that their God is so far away. They know him as God, the Father, and even as God, the Son; yet they have never really come to know him as God, the Holy Spirit. It is through his Holy Spirit that God draws nigh to us. It is the Holy Spirit, as Henry Pitt Van Dusen puts it, who is "the agency of God's self-disclosure to the individual Christian in his inmost soul." [1] Indeed, Van Dusen suggests that sometimes we need to turn the Trinitarian formula around and think of Spirit, Son, and Father. It is the Holy Spirit who convicts and converts, who leads us into an experience of the love of Christ, and who brings us into a personal knowledge of the redemptive purpose of God, the Father.

We cannot create our own overflow of blessings and power. Only God can do that. But he promises us power through his Holy Spirit. "Ye shall receive power," Jesus told the disciples, "after that the Holy Ghost is come upon you" (Acts 1:8). That promise has never been withdrawn. On the contrary, Van Dusen contends that an awareness of the Holy Spirit, his presence and his work, can become the "most exciting, enlarging, and enriching element of our faith." [2] Lest we think of an overflow of spiritual power as just a matter of personal enthusiasm or charm, let us consider the role of the Holy Spirit as an all-important factor in Christian faith and growth.

Without faith in the Holy Spirit, God can seem distant and very withdrawn. H. Wheeler Robinson discloses that once during a serious illness, he was disturbed to find that the Christian truths he had taught others did not seem to give him the spiritual strength he needed in the face of his physical weakness. It was not that he doubted their validity; he just did not seem to feel their vitality. He certainly believed in the truth of God's presence, but he was not feeling the touch of God's power. He asked himself if part of the reason might be that he had thought all too little about the presence of the Holy Spirit. So he turned to the Bible to study everything it had to teach about the Holy Spirit. The result was that after fifteen years of study, he published a book entitled *The Christian Experience of the Holy Spirit.*[3]

Many Christians today know that what they believe with their minds does not seem to energize their lives. There is a gap between that to which they give consent and that which really buoys their spirits and motivates their actions. With the study of science, God for many has seemed to recede into his vast universe. With the growth of secularism, he has been hidden from the eyes of many. Yet there is a restlessness in the world. People run about as if they are running from something. But they cannot run away from their own unhappiness and insecurity. What they need is a new experience with God. Men need a new awareness of his presence in the human heart. They need a new awareness of the Holy Spirit as the one who speaks directly to their conscience and who deals directly with their heart.

When we turn to the Bible to learn about the Holy Spirit, one thing becomes crystal clear. When we think of the Holy Spirit, we are to think of *Him*, not of *It*. Everywhere the New Testament speaks of the Holy Spirit in terms of personal attributes. The Holy Spirit thinks, he feels, he directs, he instructs, he wills. The apostle Paul tells us that the Holy Spirit prays for us "with groanings which cannot be uttered" (Rom. 8:26). He searches our hearts, says the apostle, and prays "according to the will of God" (Rom. 8:27). Jesus says the Holy Spirit is our teacher whose task is to convict the world of sin and convince men of the salvation of Christ. "He shall not speak of himself," said Jesus, "but . . . he shall glorify me: for he shall receive of mine, and shall shew it unto you. All things that the Father hath are mine," Jesus goes on to explain, "therefore said I, that he shall take of mine, and shall shew it unto you" (John 16: 13–15).

The Holy Spirit, then, is not a vague, impersonal force like school spirit or esprit de corps. He is not just the spirit of brotherhood or the spirit of good will. He is Person emanating from God, the Supreme Being, to take the things of Christ and show them unto us. "The Holy Spirit," says Edward G. Latch, "is the Spirit of God in the spirit of man. The Holy Spirit is not a wave of influence sent out from a distant creator; . . . it is God himself in the human heart; not something apart from God, but that which is a part of God."[4]

The Holy Spirit can just as truly be thought of as the Spirit of Christ. George S. Hendry writes: "There is no reference in the New Testament to any work of the [Holy] Spirit apart from Christ. The Spirit is, in an exclusive sense, the Spirit of Christ."[5]

In a sense, he can be thought of as the unifying presence in the Godhead.

How we think of the Holy Spirit makes all the difference in the world in our response to him. For, as R. A. Torrey pointed out some years ago, if we think of the Holy Spirit as *It*, then we are tempted to ask, "How can I get hold of the Holy Spirit and use it?" But if we think of the Holy Spirit as *He*, then our concern is how we can relate ourselves to him. Our question then becomes, "How can the Holy Spirit get hold of and use me?" [6]

After all, what helps us most in times of grief or loneliness— something we read in a book, or the love of a friend? What helps us most when we are tempted—to think about a law or a loved one? Many a person who has been grievously tempted has been kept from yielding to sin, not because he thought of a law that would forbid it, but because he thought of a person who would be hurt if he yielded to it.

What keeps a youth away from home from yielding to sin? Fear of consequences? That doesn't seem to deter many these days. But many a young person has been held on the right path because he thought of his mother, or his sweetheart, or the people in his church who would be hurt if they were ever to learn that he had yielded to temptation.

There is someone closer than a mother, or a sweetheart, or those in the Christian community who is hurt when we yield to sin. That someone, says Paul, is the Holy Spirit. "Grieve not the holy Spirit of God," he writes in Ephesians 4:30. Dwight L. Moody was once asked if, believing as he did, he could go to the theater. Mr. Moody replied, "I am free to go to the theater any time I want to. I just don't ever want to." We may not altogether share his attitude toward the theater, but if the Holy Spirit is *Person*—one who can be grieved by our actions—then we are led to ask, "Is where I want to go a place to which the Holy Spirit would want to accompany me? Is what I want to do something in which the Holy Spirit would want to share?" Paul speaks an arresting word when he says, "Grieve not the holy Spirit of God."

The Holy Spirit is not given to us just to keep us from doing something wrong. His power is given to us so that our lives can overflow with joy and service. When we look further to learn what the New Testament says about the Holy Spirit, we find that two things characterize his presence. Van Dusen calls those two characteristics: *intimacy* and *potency*—"God near" and "God mighty"—"God at hand" and "God at work." [7] If God, the Father, manifests the *ultimacy* of God, and God, the Son, manifests his *character;* then God, the Holy Spirit, manifests the *intimacy* of God—God in our hearts.[8]

Jesus' word for the Holy Spirit confirms this. That word has been variously translated "Comforter" and "Counselor." The literal meaning of the Greek is "one called alongside," or "one who is ready to be called alongside." Concerning this one, Jesus says, "I will pray the Father, and he shall give you *another* Comforter, that he may abide with you for ever" (John 14:16). There are two words in Greek meaning "another." One means "another of the same kind," and the other means "another of a different kind." The Greek word here means "another of the same kind." What Jesus had been to the disciples in the flesh, the Comforter, one the same as Jesus, would be to them in the spirit.

Jesus goes on to describe the Holy Spirit as one "whom the world cannot receive, because it seeth him not" (John 14:17). What did he mean? The Greek word translated "receive" means literally "to take hold of by the hand." This suggests an interesting interpretation. In a few hours, the soldiers of the high priest would arrest Jesus; they would take hold of him with their hands. They would lead him away and take him from the disciples. But they could never take hold of the Holy Spirit. They could not arrest him. They could not take him away as they had Jesus, because he is Spirit. Here, then, is a Presence—One called alongside—One the same as Jesus—One whom the world cannot arrest, or take away, who is to be our Comforter, our Counselor, forever.

How does a person become conscious of the presence of this Counselor? Those who have been most conscious of his presence attest that they have been made most aware of his nearness in times of quiet seeking. After all, if we want to appreciate great music, we must become quiet. If we want to appreciate great poetry or art, we must learn to be still. It makes sense, then, to think that we must be still to hear the whisperings of the Holy Spirit of God.

Sometimes the presence of the Holy Spirit is felt best in group experience—through group prayer and worship. Many a person had never experienced a Spirit-filled life until he became a part of a corporate quest for God's will. In a sense, this was true at Pentecost. At one point, the author of the Fourth Gospel makes the rather surprising statement that "the Holy Ghost was not yet given; because that Jesus was not yet glorified" (John 7:39). But there seems also to have been another reason why the disciples had not yet experienced the power of the Holy Spirit. At that time, they were still a lot of self-seeking, quarreling individuals. It was not until Pentecost that they were "all with one accord in one place" (Acts 2:1). When they had prayed themselves empty of self and into a living, harmonious whole, the power came with a rush "as of a rushing mighty wind" (Acts 2:2).

The Trinity, therefore, to them was not a doctrine but an experience. They had experienced what someone has called the "many-sidedness" of God. They had believed in God as the God of their fathers before they knew Jesus. Then they knew Jesus. In his life and death and especially his resurrection, they believed they saw the redemptive nature of God fully manifested. A. M. Ramsey puts it, "The most stupendous change followed the Resurrection: Hebrew monotheists, without forsaking their monotheism, worshipped Jesus as Lord." [9] Now at Pentecost they had had a new and vitalizing experience. Surely this was the power of the Holy Spirit that Jesus had promised. And so they rushed out, not to proclaim a doctrine, but to tell of an experience. The doctrine would come later to explain the experience. They had experienced God as Father, and God as Son, and now they had experienced God as Holy Spirit. Moreover, they were together when they experienced this power. It is through the interplay of two or more dedicated lives, two or more questing minds, two or more quiet and waiting hearts, that Jesus can fulfill his promise, "Where two or three are gathered together in my name, there am I in the midst of them" (Matt. 18:20).

The second characteristic of the Holy Spirit as seen in the Bible, and realized in experience, is potency. Wherever men have experienced his presence, they have felt an augmentation of power. They have felt a quickening of their natural powers —mental, spiritual, and sometimes even physical. This is exactly what Paul said the Holy Spirit would do. "But if the Spirit of him that raised up Jesus from the dead dwell in you, he that raised up Christ from the dead shall also quicken your mortal bodies by his Spirit that dwelleth in you" (Rom. 8:11). This is no empty promise. Handel was inspired to compose *The Messiah* in twenty-two days. Sallman was inspired to paint the head of Christ. Sometimes a minister is inspired to preach as if another voice were speaking through him. Strength does come to us when we need it most. We are moved to repentance for our sins. We are given strength to live the Christian life— strength that we often feel comes from beyond ourselves.

This is what happened at Pentecost. Ordinary people were enabled to make an extraordinary witness. Tongues were miraculously unloosed. National and racial differences were no longer a barrier. Those who observed it could not understand what they heard and saw. "Are not all these which speak Galileans?" they asked in amazement (Acts 2:7). This was not a compliment. In Judah, Galileans were considered to be an inferior class of people. How could these ill-regarded neighbors be capable of such a courageous and effective witness? This, as Peter contended, was a fulfilment of Joel's prophecy: "And it shall come to pass afterward, that I will pour out my spirit upon all flesh; and your sons and your daughters shall prophesy, your old men shall dream dreams, your young men shall see visions: And also upon the servants and upon the hand-maids in those days will I pour out my spirit" (Joel 2:28–29). In ancient times, kings and priests were set aside for their tasks by being anointed with oil. Now humble followers of Christ were being anointed, not with oil, but with the Holy Spirit. This was evidence, as the author of Revelation keeps repeating, that Christ "hath made us kings and priests unto God" (1:6).

Obviously, we must give the Holy Spirit something to quicken. We must give him helping hands and a willing heart. The disciples did not go out empty-handed or empty-headed. They had something to tell. They had been with Jesus. They had seen his life and death. God had raised him up from the dead. Thanks to the Bible, the church, and personal experience, we also have something to tell. We should try, with the Spirit's help, to tell it well.

A few years ago, a young student who appeared to be quite religious was asked to speak to a youth meeting. When he was presented, he said, "I always depend on the Holy Spirit to tell me what to say. He has not given me a message, so I have nothing to say to you." After he had left, the young people decided it was the student, not the Holy Spirit, who had failed. They felt he was doubly guilty because he tried to put the blame for his own laziness on the Holy Spirit. The group decided they had no right to ask the Holy Spirit to help them pass a test for which they had not studied, or to help them solve a problem about which they did not try to do their best.

In Paul's day, as in our own, there were those who associated the Holy Spirit with exaggerated emotionalism and ecstatic utterances. Paul did not minimize the place of rapture in religion. He himself claimed to have had such experiences. Our faith can help us at times to "mount up with wings as eagles." However, for the most part, we need its help to enable us to "run, and not be weary" and to "walk, and not faint" (Isa. 40:31).

The real test of the Spirit's presence, Paul insisted, is moral and ethical rather than just ethereal and ecstatic. If he mentioned ecstatic utterance at all, he put it at the end of the list as being the least important. To those who boasted of superior spirituality because they were moved to speak in tongues, Paul pointed to Christian love as "a more excellent way" (1 Cor. 12:31).

"Love, joy, peace, longsuffering, gentleness, goodness, faith, meekness, temperance"—these, says Paul, are "the fruit of the Spirit" (Gal. 5:22-23). These are given to us, Torrey reminds us, not just to make us "personally happy," or even primarily to make us "individually holy," but to make us "useful" in the kingdom of God. "There is not a single passage in the Bible," he contends, "either in the Old Testament or in the New Testament, where the baptism of the Holy Spirit is spoken of, where it is not connected with testimony and service." [10]

This is why the Holy Spirit takes the things of Christ and shows them to us—his life, his teachings, his service, his obedience, his sacrifice, his death. This is to keep us from merely believing in what someone has called the "trinity of positive thinking, peace of mind, and Pablum." This calls us back to the true Trinity of God's righteousness, love, and power as manifested in his Eternal Being, his Son, and his Holy Spirit. We may never have had an ecstatic experience. That isn't important. What is important is that the qualities of love, joy, peace, longsuffering, gentleness, goodness, faith, meekness, and temperance be seen in us. This is evidence that his Spirit has quickened us to a new awareness of the qualities demanded of us by God's righteousness and imparted to us by his love.

God will not give us more power than we are willing or able to use. A wealthy couple gave their young son a sports car upon his graduation from high school. He took the car out on the road, and as he felt the surge of power under his foot, he pushed the pedal too far. The result was a skidding crash and sudden death. God does make the mistake of giving us power that we cannot, or will not, dedicate and use to his glory. He does not give us power for our own selfish enjoyment. He calls us to serve, and often in the act of serving, the power comes to give us strength for the task. He calls us to stand firm in the face of trials that seem too great to bear, and often in standing firm, he gives us superhuman strength to stand the test. Many an obstacle that seems insurmountable in our own strength becomes a means to victory when we face it in the Lord's strength. With the psalmist we, too, are led to say, "By my God have I leaped over a wall" (18:29).

We do not achieve spiritual power. It is God's gift. We do not convict and convert. That is the work of the Holy Spirit. A minister was approached on the street by a drunkard who said, "You don't know me, do you?" The minister asked, "Should I?" The drunkard replied, "You ought to know me. I'm one of your converts." The minister looked at him sadly and said, "You must be right. You must be one of my converts. You don't look like one of the Lord's."

To believe in the Holy Spirit is to be conscious of the greatest ally in the world—not an ally to do our bidding, but one who helps us to do his. When we are tempted, the Holy Spirit is alongside to give us strength. When we turn to the Bible, the Holy Spirit is there to help us understand. When we speak to another in trouble, the Holy Spirit is already dealing with that person's heart.

Paul did not say, "I can do all things through my thoughts and my efforts which strengthen me," but "I can do all things through Christ which strengtheneth me" (Phil. 4:13). Christ is always present in the person of the Holy Spirit. To live in daily expectation of his presence and power is to have access to a well of water springing up within us. The result is an overflow of faith, service, and love to all mankind.

8.

When Enemies
Encircle

The person who wants his life to overflow with goodness and peace soon discovers that there are enemies seeking to frustrate and defeat his purpose. When the psalmist wrote, "Thou preparest a table before me in the presence of mine enemies" (23:5), he was not being paranoiac. He was stating a realistic fact. Life is a battlefield where the forces of good and evil are locked in terrible combat. There are many enemies of the Christian life. Fear or surrender has kept many a person from living a life overflowing with faith and courage.

When Leroy Campbell prayed, "Be thou my battleshield, sword for the fight," he was expressing a vital need. We not only have to cope with the cuts and bruises of suffering as we try to follow along the paths of righteousness. We also have to face formidable enemies of our faith—enemies who would defeat us and knock from our hands the overflowing cup of a radiant and faithful witness. The closer we try to follow the Good Shepherd, the more some will hate us for the things for which we stand. The cross is often the world's answer to goodness. Paul's experience at Ephesus is often repeated in the life of the Christian: "For a great door and effectual is opened unto me, and there are many adversaries" (1 Cor. 16:9).

There are many adversaries in the world today. With nuclear weapons at their disposal, peril has grown to apocalyptic proportions. But the danger is not confined to human enemies and atomic bombs. The problem is even greater than that. The same forces that turn men into our enemies also attack our own souls. There are dark forces at work in the hearts and minds of men, and it is a wise person who knows he cannot hope to conquer them alone even in himself, much less in the world. Paul reminds us: "We wrestle not against flesh and blood, but against principalities, against powers, against the rulers of the darkness of this world, against spiritual wickedness in high places" (Eph. 6:12). Against such enemies, we need the shepherd's rod—the rod of spiritual power—if we are to win out against the forces of evil in ourselves and in the world.

The enemies of Christianity and the soul do not always engage in a frontal attack. Often, they are content with sabotage. There exists the frontal attack of communism, but there is the more indirect attack of secularism which Edmund Perry defines as "life organized without God" and of materialism which he defines as "life evaluated apart from God." [1] Samuel H. Miller says:

Plainly this world is not a fool's paradise where one may wander as one will without harm or hurt. There are hostile forces at work, and the common paths of man's life are beset with perils and temptations. What makes the danger grave is that the threat is subtle. The soul may be lost by such slow degrees and socially approved activities that it disappears before one is conscious of its going.[2]

We are at the mercy of a secularized culture. Our cities are so full of cement, steel, smoke, and sin that there is little room left for spirit. Even in beautiful suburbia, landscaping takes precedence over the Lord. It is almost like talking a foreign language to say, "Except the Lord keep the city, the watchman waketh but in vain" (Psalm 127:1). What chance has the soul against the millions of dollars poured out to stimulate the sensual and glorify the material? Most people in our western culture do not argue against the existence of God, they just ignore him. They do not oppose the church, they just neglect it. The soul gets lost in the mad struggle to gain and maintain status in the social and material world.

In the battle of the soul, one's own friends and neighbors can become his enemies. One would think in a world where there is so much sin, that when one sincerely tries to live the good life, others would admire and help him. But this is not always the case. Let a person commit himself to abstinence, and scores of people will go out of their way to tempt him to drink. Let a person make a misstep, and the vultures of gossip will close in to gorge themselves on the details. A person who tries to be honest in business is thrown into competition with those who are unscrupulous. When we look into our own lives, we see how easily we become a part of the problem instead of being a part of the answer. There are enemies around us and within us with which we must do constant battle.

The Christian must try to let the spirit of goodwill overflow even in the face of real enemies. How to deal with human enemies is a problem as old as the race. The Bible is only four chapters old when we find Lamech declaring a doctrine of multiple vengeance: "If Cain shall be avenged sevenfold, truly Lamech seventy and sevenfold" (Gen. 4:24). By Moses' time, people had moved forward to the idea of equal retribution: "life for life, eye for eye, tooth for tooth, hand for hand, . . . burning for burning, . . . stripe for stripe" (Ex. 21:23–25). In this spirit, Samson justifies his acts of revenge against the Philistines by proclaiming the Golden Rule in reverse: "As they did unto me, so have I done unto them" (Judg. 15:11). The cry of revenge from a hurt and resentful heart probably reaches its zenith in the psalmist's cry against the cruel captors of the Israelites: "Happy shall he be, that taketh and dasheth thy little ones against the stones" (137:9).

Similar bitter resentment is voiced even by some of the disciples of Jesus who gave vent to their anger against a Samaritan village that had refused them entrance by asking,

"Lord, wilt thou that we command fire to come down from heaven, and consume them?" (Luke 9:54). Such an attitude today could lead to the complete destruction of civilization. It is now literally possible for man himself to rain down from heaven fire that will consume not just one village but whole cities. Such a poisoning of the atmosphere over millions of square miles of earth would thus endanger the lives of hundreds of thousands, who could not by any stretch of the imagination be considered our enemies.

Against this dark background of retaliation and revenge, Proverbs 25:21–22 stands out like a surprising shaft of light: "If thine enemy be hungry, give him bread to eat; and if he be thirsty, give him water to drink: For thou shalt heap coals of fire upon his head, and the Lord shall reward thee." These verses receive additional emphasis because Paul quotes them in the twelfth chapter of Romans (v. 20). Taking issue with the old idea of retributive justice, Paul says, "Recompense to no man evil for evil . . . avenge not yourselves, but rather give place unto wrath: for it is written, Vengeance is mine; I will repay, saith the Lord" (vv. 17,19). In other words, we can leave the problem of punishment up to God. He, and he alone, knows how to deal with it with perfect justice and love. Paul's teaching is not an easy one. He indicates this by his qualifying statement, "If it be possible, . . . live peaceably with all men" (v. 18). Paul goes on to sum up his suggested approach by saying, "Be not overcome of evil, but overcome evil with good" (v. 21).

At this point, Paul was simply reflecting Jesus' difficult teaching, "Love your enemies, bless them that curse you, do good to them that hate you, and pray for them which despitefully use you, and persecute you" (Matt. 5:44).

There are two ways to try to get rid of an enemy. One is to destroy the enemy; the other is to destroy his enmity. The first usually creates new enemies in the process and does nothing to solve the problem of hate in the heart of the avenger. The second turns the enemy into a friend. The first can be done by bullets or snubs; the second can only be done by love and understanding. Love is the only force that has a chance of turning an enemy into a friend.

Important as this is, it is still not the basis on which Jesus rested his teaching. He did not urge us to love our enemies because of what it may do for them—they may go right on being our enemies—but because of what it will do for us. It will keep us from stooping to the level of spite and hate. It will make us feel and act more like the children of God who makes his sun "to rise on the evil and on the good, and sendeth rain on the just and on the unjust" (Matt. 5:45). We are obviously a long way from achieving this goal in personal and international relations, but the peace of the world depends upon our moving in that direction.

The Christian must also face up to enmity and sin in his own heart. The problem gets close to us when we think of how to deal with the spirit of enmity in our own heart, and how to face up to the problem of man's enmity toward God. One's soul is a battleground where good and evil struggle, where evil forces seek to take him captive and destroy his loyalty to the Heavenly King. However we try to explain it, there is in the universe that which rebels against God, and seeks to plant this spirit of rebellion in our own hearts.

Sin is our greatest enemy. The Bible constantly tries to alert us to its insidious nature and the seriousness of its menace. Sin, it points out, is universal in its corrupting influence: "All we like sheep have gone astray; we have turned every one to his own way" (Isa. 53:6). Sin is fatal to spiritual aspiration and hope: "The wages of sin is death" (Rom. 6:23). Sin is rapacious in its appetite: "Your adversary the devil, as a roaring lion, walketh about, seeking whom he may devour" (1 Peter 5:8).

Unfortunately, the devil doesn't look like a lion. If he did, it would scare us off. Paul accurately describes how temptation confronts us when he says Satan appears as an "angel of light" (Moffatt translates it "masquerades," 2 Cor. 11:14). In other words, sin is attractive on the surface or we wouldn't be tempted. It promises what it cannot deliver. It promises gladness and delivers guilt. It promises life and leads to spiritual death. But it usually does it in such a subtle way. We are seldom tempted to leap into hell in one jump. "Just this once," the tempter pleads. What an advantage any sin has gained over us if our resistance can be broken down to where we will take the first step. We are not asked to be drunkards. Such a thought would be repulsive to us. We are asked to take just one drink to be sociable. We are not asked to hate the church— just to stay at home when it is not convenient for us to make the effort to attend until gradually we lose interest.

As if it were not enough to face real dangers to the soul, we are often deprived of moral courage by being tempted to conjure up imaginary ones. With keen psychological insight, the author of Proverbs says, "The slothful man saith, There is a lion without" (22:13). Or, as one modern scholar translates it, "The lazy man sits idle; he says there might be a lion outside." By this means we are induced into cowardly inactivity or silence by dangers we ourselves have imagined. Raindrops can look like lion's teeth to many church members on Sunday. A person who is talkative at his club can suddenly become tongue-tied when it is necessary to defend someone who is being unjustly criticized, or when he needs to speak up on behalf of his religious faith. The fear of appearing foolish or too saintly looms up like an angry lion to force the words back down his throat. If only men were as quick to detect real dangers to spiritual stature as they are to imagine dangers to their social standing, there would be more moral courage in the world and more soldiers in the fight for truth and right.

A Christian must learn to look at sin through God's eyes. If, as Paul puts it, we are to "withstand in the evil day, and having done all, to stand" (Eph. 6:13), we must know how to penetrate sin's disguises and recognize its diabolical nature. What is sin? What makes a thought or act sinful? Psychologist J. A. Hadfield gives the clue when he says, "Evil is not a thing, but a wrong function; it is the use of a good impulse at the wrong time, in the wrong place, towards a wrong end, that constitutes an evil function." [3] It is taking a God-given means and making it an end in itself. It is substituting human desire for reverence for personality and devotion to the will of God. It is like taking a lovely tapestry that has been given to us for the adornment of our home and using it as a towel on which to wipe our dirty hands. It is, says Carl Sumner Knopf, the making of "choices that serve self at the expense of others, or animal instincts at the expense of men's higher possibilities." [4] It is taking sex and turning it into lust, thirst and turning it into intemperance, hunger and turning it into gluttony. But why is this wrong? It is wrong not only because it degrades personality, but because it violates God's purpose in giving these gifts to us in the first place. In the last analysis, sin is a defiance of God. It is, says E. Stanley Jones, "an attempt to break the laws of God and get away with it."

But we don't get away with it. Look at the world and see. See the greed, of which we are not entirely free, on every hand. Observe the black clouds of prejudice and hate blotting out the sun of understanding and justice. See sex cheapened and exploited as perhaps it has not been since the licentious days of the Roman empire. Look at corruption so widespread that one sometimes wonders whether anyone is thoroughly honest any more. All this and more is the result of man's sin— sin to which each of us has in some measure contributed.

In addition to the enemies of the moral life, there are enemies to a satisfying devotional life. These enemies not only would try to drive us away from God but would try to prevent us from drawing near to him. The cause may be, and often is, a seemingly harmless thing. It may be laziness, or just drowsiness. It is significant that in Jesus' story of the wheat and the tares, the enemy sowed tares in the field while the man who had sowed good seed slept. It was sleep that kept the disciples from watching with Jesus during his trying hour in Gethsemane. Many a person who would not think of missing church will, time and again, permit drowsiness to rob him of a vital worship experience. Sometimes the difficulty is an uninspiring service, an overheated room, or an overfull stomach. Sometimes it is just lack of interest and attention. Whatever it is, it dulls our sensitivity to the presence of God. Someone has said that the tragedy of Rip Van Winkle is that he slept through the American Revolution with a loaded musket by his side and never fired a single shot. Drowsiness can turn Christian disciples into spiritual Rip Van Winkles, sleeping with the weapon of prayer by their sides while all the world is caught in the throes of revolution. This is one reason for finding time in the early hours of the morning, when one is rested and his day is usually at its best, for quiet communion with God.

There are distractions of all kinds when we try to concentrate our attention on God. John Donne, dramatic preacher and poet of the sixteenth century, stated this problem quite graphically when he said:

When we consider with a religious seriousnesse the manifold weaknesses of the strongest devotions in time of Prayer, it is a sad consideration. I throw my selfe downe in my Chamber, and I call in, and invite God, and his Angels thither, and when they are there, I neglect God and his Angels, for the noise of a Flie, for the ratling of a Coach, for the whining of a doore; I talke on, in the same posture of praying; Eyes lifted up; knees bowed downe; as though I prayed to God; and, if God, or his Angels should aske me, when I thought last of God in that prayer, I cannot tell: Sometimes I finde that I had forgot what I was about, but when I began to forget it, I cannot tell. A memory of yesterdays pleasures, a feare of to morrows dangers, a straw under my knee, a noise in mine eare, a light in mine eye, an any thing, a nothing, a fancy, a Chimera in my braine, troubles me in my prayer. So certainely is there nothing, nothing in spirituall things, perfect in this world.[5]

Almost anything can serve to distract us and divert our minds from God when we are trying to meditate and pray. To a friend who worried about the way his mind wandered in prayer, Brother Lawrence wrote, "You tell me nothing new; you are not the only one that is troubled with wandering thoughts. Our mind is extremely roving; but as the will is mistress of all our faculties, she must recall them, and carry them to God as their last end."[6]

Another enemy of spiritual growth is self-deception. Emily Herman says, "The most formidable enemy of the spiritual life, and the last to be conquered, is self-deception."[7] In his book, *Prayer Can Change Your Life,* William R. Parker says it is difficult even in prayer to be completely honest with ourselves and God. We want to appear at our best even in our own eyes—especially in our own eyes—and so we make excuses for ourselves even when we talk to God in prayer. Moreover, we may not know what some of our deep psychological needs may be. The psalmist prayed, "Cleanse thou me from secret faults" (19:12). They may be so secret that only God knows what they are. But he does know, and if we are faithful in bringing our lives before him and seeking his will, he can help us to know ourselves. We can thus experience more of the transforming power of his love.

Against these and all other enemies of the soul, we need spiritual protection if we are to live a life overflowing with courage and faith. Paul likens this protection to a suit of armor. Sitting in the cell of a Roman prison where daily he could see and hear the clank of Roman armor, he was inspired to write about the "whole armour of God" (Eph. 6:13).

He begins with the belt or girdle of truth. Just as in writing to the Christians at Philippi, the first virtue about which he asked them to think was truth—"Whatsoever things are true" (Phil. 4:8).

This is the right place to begin. We cannot be saved by faith in a lie. God is not only love, he is truth. If this is so, we had better obey him. Nothing else can hold our world together in peace and security. If the world is his and he made it, then his laws must run it. We cannot substitute our own ideas and expect them to work. If his way is truth, it is easy to understand what is wrong with our world. We have been trying to run it on man's conception of what is true and what will work. We have trusted in bombs more than Bibles, hate more than love. As a result, man has become enslaved in his own indulgence, pride, hate, and fear. What he needs for deliverance is to get back to the truth of God as explained in the Bible and revealed fully through him who said, "If ye continue in my word . . . ye shall know the truth, and the truth shall make you free" (John 8:31–32).

For further protective armor, Paul suggests the breastplate of righteousness. This protects the heart. Most people fail to realize how much protection a righteous life can give, but it is immeasurable. A clear conscience is the best protection one can have against the false charges of the world. When tongues begin to wag and critics would do us harm, there is no better shield than a reputation for righteous living.

A recent newspaper article told of an attempt by would-be character assassins to discredit a certain congressman. Angered by some of his congressional investigations, they had sent an agent into the congressman's home district to try to uncover some evidence of improper conduct that could be used against the lawmaker. But the search was a failure. Though they could disagree with his political views and judgments, though they could fear and resent his congressional investigations, they could find no evidence of moral or political misconduct that could be used against him. His Christian family life, his reputation for integrity in office served as an invisible protection against those who would besmirch his character and destroy his career as a public servant.

Next, if we are to live an overflowing life, we need the helmet of salvation. When Satan cannot get through to the heart, he often aims at the head. If he can get one to doubt sufficiently, he does not have to corrupt his morals to achieve his goal, which is to separate us from God. So he tries to make faith seem illogical, unreasonable and to attack us at the point of our intellectual pride. He doesn't have to make us hate God—just doubt his existence. He doesn't have to make us hate the church—just doubt its importance. He doesn't have to make us antagonistic to the Bible—just doubt its relevance. Against these dangers, Paul suggests the protection of the helmet of salvation.

We might have expected Paul to suggest the helmet of reason or logic. These are important in grappling with doubt, and some people come to discipleship mainly along the intellectual path. But Paul knew what he was saying. We do not prove God with our arguments. We trust him and let him prove himself by his saving power in our lives. The final answer to doubt is not an argument but an experience. In the area of Christian truth, example is more convincing than debate.

The apprentice who worked alongside William Carey did not have Carey's intellectual keenness, but he was a devoted Christian. He finally influenced Carey to find a deeper Christian experience. "He could not answer my questions," said Carey, "but I could not answer his life." When Jesus healed the man born blind, the man could not answer the many objections raised by the Pharisees, but neither could he discount his own experience. "Whether he be a sinner or no,

I know not: one thing I know, that, whereas I was blind, now I see" (John 9:25). One cannot refute evidence like that. To friends who taunted him about his belief in miracles, one man quietly pointed to the miracle Christian faith had wrought in his own life and home. There was his protection against derision and doubt. In the light of such evidence, the attack on its credulity fell harmlessly to the ground.

But *our* righteousness, *our* experience is not enough. We must have faith in *God's* righteousness and in *his* goodness. The breastplate of our righteousness is much too inadequate. We need the shield of faith in God's power and righteousness. This, "above all," Paul says we must have. Only faith can give us adequate protection against the enemies of the spiritual life—faith not in our power but in God's power. We cannot claim victory through our goodness, but through his. The source of our confidence is not our merit, but his grace. And the source of our assurance is the cross. This must be the emblem on our shield of faith. For at the cross sin was at its worst. But at the cross sin more than met its match. In Christ the powers of sin and death have been defeated. Sin was no equal for him. Because of his resurrection, death is no longer our greatest enemy. We fight under the banner of the conqueror of sin and death.

Each Easter in the John Wanamaker store in Philadelphia, there is displayed Michael Munkacsy's great painting of the crucifixion. In the foreground of the canvas there is a young man who had started to run away from the cross. Evidently he had started to run toward Jerusalem to tell his friends about the crucifixion. But something—evidently a cry from the cross—has stopped him in his tracks. He is half turned around, his arms partly extended. One foot still points in the direction in which he had started to run, but his face is turned back toward the cross.

His stance is symbolic. Hardly had the followers of Jesus

left the scene of the crucifixion until they were looking back at the cross in wonderment and faith. Instead of saying God was defeated, they were soon saying that never in history had God spoken so clearly to proclaim his redemptive purpose and love. Instead of trying to forget the cross, they were saying, "For I determined not to know any thing among you, save Jesus Christ, and him crucified" (1 Cor. 2:2). Instead of explaining away its reproach, they gloried in it and considered it an honor to share it: "Wherefore Jesus also, that he might sanctify the people with his own blood, suffered without the gate. Let us go forth therefore unto him without the camp, bearing his reproach" (Heb. 13:12–13). The cross had become the greatest moral influence in their lives and their greatest reason for believing in the redemptive power and purpose of God.

With such a gospel, the Christian dare not withdraw from the world's challenge. "Shod with the preparation of the gospel of peace" (Eph. 6:15), he must go forth to declare it, carrying with him "the sword of the Spirit, which is the word of God" (Eph. 6:17)—a weapon that is "sharper than any twoedged sword" (Heb. 4:12), that can cut between truth and error, and can even expose to view the innermost thoughts and intents of the heart. By the truth of this word, we can overcome. Even so, the dangers are constant. We must, says Paul, be constantly alert in prayer, "watching thereunto with all perseverance" (Eph. 6:18), that we may protect ourselves from, and defeat, the enemies of the soul.

Equipped with such a faith in our divine leader and his cause, we are made "more than conquerors" (Rom. 8:37). But many a conqueror has not been able to conquer himself or his own ruthless passions and ambitions. All Europe once trembled at the step of Napoleon. As he gained victory after victory, his little, timid mother kept repeating to her friends, *"Pourvu que cela dure"*—"If it only lasts." But it didn't last.

With God's help, however, we can win victory over ourselves, be encouraged to fight for truth and right, and claim the promise, that if we stand with him who is the conqueror of death, that one day we will share the victory that lasts forever. Then, with the table of eternity prepared before us, we can eat of its bounty in peace, for we will no longer be in the presence of our enemies.

9.
When Trouble Comes

James Moffatt translates Acts 14:22 to read, "We have to get into the Realm of God through many a trouble." Sooner or later, we run into this disturbing truth. Jesus' life did not stop overflowing with love when he reached Golgotha. Indeed, it overflowed the more. Much as men felt his love when he taught them on the mountainside, they felt it more as he cried for their forgiveness from the cross.

If we want a life overflowing with faith and power, we cannot stop with the twenty-third Psalm. We must go on to the forty-second, the fifty-first, the eighty-fourth. Psalm 23, most people would agree, presents a rather serene and uncomplicated picture of faith. There is no wrestling with guilt as in Psalm 51, no loneliness as in Psalm 84, no hint that faith must win out over despair as in Psalm 42. One suspects the psalmist was living in untroubled days when he painted this appealing picture of a serene and confident faith. The phrase, "My cup runneth over," would suggest that it was a time of abundant blessings. This, in turn, led to a quiet confidence in the future: "Surely goodness and mercy shall follow me all the days of my life." True, the thought of death casts a shadow across the psalmist's mind, and enemies lurk off the edge of the picture, but God's presence and protecting rod are more than adequate for these dangers. For the most part, the skies in the twenty-third Psalm are sunny and clear.

But what happens when the storms begin to blow? What about confidence in God's goodness when life hands us experi-

102

ences that seem to be anything but an expression of goodness? What do we do when, for the time being, the whirling sands of trouble and despair seem to obscure the Shepherd's face? How do we hold the cup with a steady hand when it overflows with sorrow? How shall we sing the Lord's song in the strange land of tragedy and pain? It is very evident to anyone who looks around him, or who has lived very long, that we need an adequate faith for these trying times. The world is not just one big, happy family. Life is not just one big bed of roses. Sin is still real. Pain is still pain. Dictators still threaten the peace. Men can be cruel as well as kind. Sometimes life itself can seem terribly cruel as we experience suffering or, harder still, watch someone we love suffer very much.

When the inevitable tests and trials come, how can we find adequate spiritual resources with which to acquit ourselves creditably? To use Isaiah's phrase—when we pass through the rivers, how can we share his confidence that they shall not overflow us? When we walk through the fire, how can we know that we shall not be burned? For we do sometimes walk through deep waters, and the fires of suffering can test our souls. This is why, in addition to an awareness of God's goodness, we need faith in his mercy. We do sin and need forgiveness. We do suffer and need his comforting strength.

It was for just such times as these that much of the Bible was written. This is not a false portrayal of human experience. The Bible talks more about persecution than pleasure. It tells of trials as well as triumphs, war as well as peace, sin as well as salvation, death as well as birth. There is no false optimism here about human nature. It is clear that men are worth saving or Jesus would not have given his life to save them, but he gave his life to save them because they need to be saved. "If ye then, being evil," was the way he stated humanity's problem (Matt. 7:11). The Bible presents no little conception of sin, or of God's power to deal with it. It portrays a God whose judgments we cannot escape, but whose grace is sufficient for all of our needs. The Bible also warns against self-righteousness, and it exposes the utter inadequacy of self-sufficiency as a way of life. Like the bed of which Isaiah warned, self-reliance is "shorter than that a man can stretch himself on it" (28:20). Man is also warned against trusting in material things. They are a covering "narrower than that he can wrap himself in it" (v. 20). Full barns are no help when God says, "This night thy soul shall be required of thee" (Luke 12:20).

Yet, we go around with abundant faith in ourselves and little conceptions of God. Learning that Miss Suzanne Rinck was a Bible teacher, a young man said to her, "Pretty soon we're going to reach the moon. What will you do with your Bible then?" What a strange question to ask, and what a limited knowledge of biblical truth it reveals. God is not something man can outdistance by going to the moon, not someone who can be left behind in earthly temples. God's power does not stop at the limits of the earth's atmosphere. How does the young man think the moon, the stars, and the laws by which their movements are governed got there in the first place?

Man will not lose his need for faith in God merely by entering outer space. A knowledge of how to reach the moon will not change human nature or erase the problem of human suffering. It will only increase our fear of interplanetary war. It will not cancel out sin and temptation. Men can be greedy and hate each other on the moon as much as on the earth. It will not change the fact of death. The first lunar cosmonaut had better take a Bible with him. He may sense the need of God's presence there more than he ever thought he needed it on the earth.

Our problem, however, is not what happens when man reaches the moon. Our problem is what happens here when serious sickness comes, when death invades the family circle, when sin or loneliness overwhelms, or when some other grave crisis leaves us, temporarily at least, stunned. Where can we find the faith to go on, the faith to turn disaster into victory, the faith to believe in God's goodness when green pastures seem, for the time being, to be a mocking mirage? How can we have a faith that overflows with confidence even in the midst of trials? Must we surrender faith in the goodness of God, or can we, even in the valley of the shadow, feel his presence?

The time to consider such questions is not when the crisis comes and we are stunned, but when we can approach the Lord in calmness of spirit. The prophet says, "Seek ye the Lord while he may be found" (Isa. 55:6). God may be found at all times, but we can recognize his voice more quickly in the darkness if we have learned to talk with him in the light.

Some years ago, on a popular radio program known as the Seth Parker Hour, this story was told. Silas Mathews and Seth Parker were riding behind a fine team of spirited horses. Silas Mathews was holding the reins. Something happened to frighten the horses, and they began to run away downhill. Fearful for his life, Silas Mathews dropped the reins, grabbed the side of the wagon, and began to pray for dear life. Seeing what was happening, Seth Parker grabbed the reins, and as he pulled the horses to a stop, he yelled out of the side of his mouth, "Silas, you're too far behind in your praying installments to get caught up now. I'm caught up in mine. I'm ready to go into action."

What was this story trying to say? For one thing, it was saying that the picture of life can change with dramatic suddenness. We make our long-range plans, and overnight sickness comes, or an accident occurs with sickening impact, or a loved one is taken from us, and all our carefully laid plans are brought to a shattering end. Or, like the author of the fifty-fifth Psalm, we trust a friend and he betrays us; someone in whom "the words of his mouth were smoother than butter, but war was in his heart" (v. 21). We struggle to save, and an unforeseen emergency wipes out our savings. We build our dream castles, and suddenly they lie in ruins at our feet.

While the picture of life may change in a minute's time, the habits and faiths of a lifetime are not apt to change so quickly. The thing to do, therefore, is not to wait until the crisis comes, and then cry out in panic, "Lord, where are you?" If we have walked with him by faith, we will know where he is. He is by our side. He is in our heart. He will help us as we go into action. We will not even waste time crying out, "Why?" We will know that just as the Heavenly Father "maketh his sun to rise on the evil and on the good, and sendeth rain on the just and the unjust" (Matt. 5:45), so sorrow, sickness, and trouble come to the good as well as the bad. Sickness is no respecter of persons. Death comes to rich and poor, saint and sinner, alike. The difference, of course, is in how we face up to what happens to us. The Bible nowhere promises exemption from suffering as a reward for being good. It warns that faith can lead to greater suffering through persecution. But it does point to a faith that can turn even suffering into spiritual gain.

Paul gives the answer of a man of faith. "We know," he writes, "that in everything God works for good with those who love him" (Rom. 8:28, RSV). Paul is not saying that everything that happens to us is good. That could hardly be said about many of life's tragic ills. He is saying, however, that nothing can happen to us from which good may not come, if we have a strong enough faith in God and are sufficiently committed to his will. This is more than a "grin-and-bear-it" or "keep-your-chin-up" kind of philosophy. It is more than a grim defiance of circumstances that boasts, "My head is bloody but unbowed." This is more than stolid fatalism that says, "Into each life some rain must fall, and I'll show I can take mine along with the best of them." It is faith that puts even our suffering into the hands of God that he may use it to our good and his glory. This is the recognition that in his wisdom even suffering and sorrow have their purpose, and can become a prelude to a higher good. It is realizing that suffering can increase our sympathetic understanding, and make us grope for the hand of God in a way that we might never have done if the days had remained sunny and bright.

God has provided more than one way by which our spirits may be strengthened and our heart's hunger fed. There are green pastures of inspiration and pleasure. But even when we are away from the verdant hills, God prepares a table before us and provides an overflowing cup. Let us consider, then, some of the ways God prepares a table before us even in the presence of trials and danger.

First of all, the person who wants his life to overflow with joy even in the midst of sorrow will find a work to do. A work-bench often becomes a means of grace, a special table set before us. Busy hands can ease an aching heart, and hours of labor can become a genuine source of solace. Happiness is not to be found in the absence of work, but in finding and doing a work one wants to do. Far from being a punishment, the psalmist had discovered that work is a source of blessing and fulfilment. "Establish thou the work of our hands upon us," he prayed, "yea, the work of our hands establish thou it" (Psalm 90:17). Work is not just a means of making a living, but one of the ways God has provided for fulfilling a life.

"Blessed is he who has found his work," wrote Thomas Carlyle, "let him ask no other blessedness." While most of us would not want to settle for work as the sole blessing, we do recognize that work for which one has the aptitude and training can provide one of life's chief sources of satisfaction. "Achievement," says Ernest Ligon, "is the strongest innate source of pleasure." [1] A sense of achievement in one's work can give a person a sense of satisfaction that few things can match.

No one has to tell a born preacher to preach. He would be unhappy if he could not do so. No one has to tell an inventor to invent. God has planted that desire in his heart. Once, when his wife asked him where he would rather go than any other place in the world, Thomas Edison replied, "My laboratory."

A person's work takes on its deepest meaning when one thinks of it as a way of working with God. Not everyone can pursue what he wants to do. If it is a work that needs to be done, however, and if one joins his life in partnership with God, "even those who are not allowed to do what they crave," says Nels Ferre, "can hear in the prison of circumstance a midnight song of deliverance." [2] Thus one can find some of the satisfaction described by Maud Slye, famous research scientist, when upon her retirement she wrote:

> So many roads that go!
> My feet were set upon the service path,
> Whose glory of the day is toil,
> Whose peace at nightfall is the peace of dreams
> That reach beyond the stars!
> Whose golden trumpet call
> Is to the service of a higher toil.
> O accolade of work folded away
> And finished! It was for me to know the lonely feet,
> The weary hands—but oh the peace within my heart.[3]

Notice her reference to "lonely" feet. A second way by which God blesses our lives, and strengthens us for the tasks ahead, is through the blessing of human friends. The person who wants his life to overflow with gratitude and peace even in the face of grave trials will cherish his friends, remembering the biblical injunction, "A man that hath friends must shew himself friendly" (Prov. 18:24).

The apostle Paul was on his way up the Appian highway to Rome. If ever a man had a right to be discouraged, surely it was he. He had just been shipwrecked. He was being taken to

Rome to stand trial on a charge of which he was not guilty. Paul was no longer a young man. He had suffered privations, physical torture, misunderstandings, vile abuse, and the most vicious kind of calumny for preaching his faith. Now he was being led in chains under guard. Suddenly when they reached the point where stood the "Appii forum, and The three taverns," they met a group of Christians who had come down from Rome to greet Paul. Luke tells us that when Paul saw them "he thanked God, and took courage" (Acts 28:15).

Who has not at times, like Paul, had to draw strength and courage from his friends? A pleasure shared is a pleasure doubled. A trial shared is one more easily faced. Even Jesus wanted someone to watch with him in Gethsemane. What sadness and disappointment are echoed in his words spoken over the sleeping disciples: "What, could ye not watch with me one hour?" (Matt. 26:40). For many a young person, loneliness has been a steppingstone to trouble. One turns to the wrong crowd, not because he is bad, but because he is lonely, and fellowship is offered. For an older person who has outlived many of his friends, and perhaps his life's companion, loneliness can be his greatest problem.

This is where the church is in a unique position to serve. Since the church is supposed to draw no lines of distinction, it is in a position to welcome all who will respond to the Saviour's love, uniting them in a fellowship of faith and hope. Asked how she liked a new community into which she had moved, a woman replied with feeling, "I hate it." Lonely for old friends, she was hesitant about making new ones. Yet there was a church one block from where she lived. If the church had known her need, if she had given the people of the church the chance, they could have welcomed her into a Christian fellowship that surely would have melted some of the bitterness of her heart.

There come times in every person's life when he must go

through some dark Gethsemane alone. No one, not even a wife or husband, can go along. One must suffer his pain alone; no one can suffer it for him. One must make some decision alone; no one can make it for him. Ultimately, one must die alone. At such times, he needs the greatest friend of all who can always be touched with the feeling of our infirmities, for he "was in all points tempted like as we are, yet without sin" (Heb. 4:15). One who would have a faith overflowing with genuine assurance must seek an understanding of that Friend that appeals to his mind. He must have an experience of divine love that speaks to his heart.

First, in those moments when we stand alone and must find our spiritual resources from deep within ourselves, we need an understanding of faith that is acceptable to the mind. Faith, to be strong, must be reasonable. Faith, of course, goes beyond reason but is not antagonistic to it. It draws on all that science and philosophy can tell us about life around us. Faith, as Harnack reminds us, is not belief "in spite of evidence." Faith examines all the evidence possible and goes on from there. The scientist looks at life and describes what seems to be a law of nature. The philosopher tries to probe the meaning of the law and its relationship to all of life. The man of faith goes back of the law to its Creator whom he learns to trust, letting his experience tell him whether he is right or wrong in such trust.

This need for an understanding of faith calls for a careful study of the Bible. It is not enough to quote passages of Scripture. We must know what those passages mean. We must know what they meant when they were written. Good commentaries are a necessary part of a growing Christian's equipment. They were written by people who have made the Bible, or portions of it, a lifelong study. The simple man of faith has much to learn from the scholar. The scholar can take him behind words to discover their original meaning. He can help one to understand the context that throws light on the text. But we cannot stop there. We must know what the Bible means for us today. At that point, the Holy Spirit, not the scholar, is our final teacher. At that point, too, the scholar must become a simple man of faith. It is not enough to know about the Bible. We must learn to trust it and live by its message. We must know its Author who has inspired its unity, and speaks from its pages. No one person or group knows all the answers. All must keep on seeking, and each must help the other.

Even as we seek for more complete answers to our questions about life and about God, we would do well to remember a word spoken by F. R. Barry. Men will embrace a religion, he contends, even if it contains intellectual misgivings, *if* it "satisfies their emotional needs and proves itself in the test of moral effectiveness." [4] This is our deepest need of all—a faith that satisfies the heart and lifts us to new heights of moral grandeur. No mere religion of law can do this. Even a perfect example, as important as that is, is not enough. This calls for what William Carey called "experiential religion." It calls for a faith that stirs and changes the heart. It calls for a God who involves himself with us in our need. It calls for a response of faith and love to the God of that involvement.

This is where the message of the cross becomes so indispensible. If God were only a remote being, sitting high on a cloud, meditating on the problem of human suffering, we could not stand it. We would not feel drawn to such a God. In times of real suffering, such a God would repel, not attract, us. But the cross reveals no mere contemplative God. It means much to us in hours of sorrow to know that God himself suffered as his Son hung in undeserved agony on the cross. Indeed, if the doctrine of the incarnation is true—and how else can we explain Jesus' life and mission?—God was in that suffering. It was his idea, because there was no other way to show his righteousness and love fully to the world except through a life that would be obedient unto death. The Christian's Saviour is not one who merely meditated under a tree. He died on a tree; he involved himself in our struggle and took upon himself the "chastisement of our peace" (Isa. 53:5). "Surely he hath borne our griefs, and carried our sorrows" (Isa. 53:4). In a small way our trials make it possible for us to enter with him into the fellowship of suffering.

But if it means much to know that God understands our suffering because he himself suffered, it means everything to know that the cross did not defeat him. Caiaphas and Pilate were not the final victors. Far from being a symbol of despair, the cross has become mankind's greatest reason for believing in the love of God. The crucifixion is not the last chapter in the story. The final word concerning Jesus is not "He is dead," but "He is risen."

In the light of this revelation, the Christian faith gathers up our experiences, including our suffering, and considers them in the light of eternity. "For I reckon," declared Paul, "that the sufferings of this present time are not worthy to be compared with the glory which shall be revealed in us" (Rom. 8:18). This is our hope, and this is our incentive for Christian living—a hope that is based on the experience of the one who walked through Calvary's pain and death's dark valley to emerge triumphant in the sunlight of the resurrection morning.

As we have seen, we do not stay in the valley forever—whether it be the valley of suffering, or sorrow, or death. We walk *through* the valley into the sunshine on the other side. Life is not all shadows. The sunshine returns, and we are able to know that we have had his presence all along. If, in some small measure, our suffering reveals to us our own lack of self-sufficiency and our dependence upon God; if, knowing our weakness, we turn to him for strength; if, through suffering, we get insights that lead to a deeper surrender; then our answer will come, and his face will be revealed through the storm. Then, like Paul, we can begin to understand the promise, "My grace is sufficient for thee" (2 Cor. 12:9). Our lives will overflow with a joy that shines through our tears, and with a faith that pulsates even in the midst of our trials.

10.
The Final Gift

When Jesus sat by Jacob's well talking with a woman of Samaria, his promise of "living water" to quench the thirst of man for spiritual certainty had no time limits. It was guaranteed not only for this life but was also to be "a well of water springing up *into everlasting life*" (John 4:14).

When the author of the twenty-third Psalm counted his blessings, he was able to say with gratitude, "My cup runneth over." Green pastures, still waters, guidance for right paths, confidence of companionship for the valley of the shadow, a staff to draw him back, a rod to give him protection, food, and drink even in the presence of his enemies—these all added up to a life overflowing with manifold blessings. And the final blessing of all, the one to which all the others led, was an eternal home: "I will dwell in the house of the Lord for ever."

This was a tremendous leap of faith for the psalmist to take. This is a high-water mark of Old Testament belief in the goodness and mercy of God. Not all the Old Testament writers shared this confidence. The author of the sixth Psalm, for example, had said, "In death there is no remembrance of thee: in the grave who shall give thee thanks?" (v. 5). But the author of Psalm 23 had been given the faith to say, "Yea, though I walk through the valley of the shadow of death, I will fear no evil: for thou art with me." This stands alongside Job's great affirmation, "I know that my redeemer liveth, and that he shall stand at the latter day upon the earth: And though after my skin worms destroy this body, yet in my flesh shall I see God: Whom I shall see for myself, and mine eye shall behold, and not another" (19:25–27). Thus Job had answered his own question, "If a man die, shall he live again?" (14:14). A literal translation of the question would be, "Shall he go on living?"

Perhaps no doctrine can enable us to face the perishability of life with a greater overflow of peace and confidence than a belief in the immortality of the soul. For the Christian, this belief is expressed in the doctrine of the resurrection. Yet Job's question still lurks in our minds, even in the minds of the young. When the body dies, does the soul die with it? During World War II, a young American G.I. sat in his pastor's study. He was home for what would probably be his last furlough before being sent overseas. Soon he might be in combat areas where his life would be in grave danger. As he talked with his pastor, he said, "I don't think I would mind going quite so much, if I could really be sure that, if I didn't come back, that wouldn't be the end of me."

Job's question is not one to be filed away until death itself gives us the answer. What we believe about the solution to this question determines in large measure how we look at life here and now. We need a faith in life after death if this life is to overflow with assurance and joy. The cup of blessing becomes a cup of despair if we think that at death it is to be knocked from our grasp forever. Charles A. Ellwood says, "Human life can be lived rightly only when it is lived under the aspect of eternity." [1] It makes a tremendous difference in our attitude toward life whether we think of this existence as the whole performance or only the rehearsal; whether we think of death as the final coda, or of life as the tuning up stage that determines how God shall fit us into the symphony of eternity. A belief in life after death does much to ease our grief when our loved ones are taken from us. Our sense of frustration and despair is taken away if we can believe that death is the gateway to larger fulfilment, love triumphant, and life everlasting.

Many contend that a belief in immortality has been made more difficult by the scientific interpretation of the universe. It is true that no astronomer has been able to fix the location of heaven in the sights of his telescope. But is heaven the kind of a place that can be discovered by a telescopic lens? A belief in immortality does not seem to appear too important to many today who are engrossed in our materialistic culture. For them the blessings of this life seem so great and attractive that this dims their desire for heaven and the spiritual life.

We do not prove eternal life by argument or experiment. There is no tangible evidence that we can bring into a scientific laboratory to be weighed or measured. We must derive our belief from what we know about life itself. We know, for example, that energy can be changed but cannot be destroyed. If a piece of wood is burned in the fire, every atom that was in that wood is still in the universe in some form or other. If it is true that energy cannot be destroyed, is it beyond reason to believe that souls cannot be destroyed either? Is it reasonable to think that the chemicals of which the human body is formed go on existing after the body itself has decomposed, but that the life and personality that gave the body its significance and individuality are snuffed out forever? Does the universe keep only the materials of which the house is made and destroy the occupant? "If," says Harry Emerson Fosdick, "death ends personality, the universe seems to be throwing away with utter heedlessness its most precious possessions."[2] Professor Palmer of Harvard echoed that same thought when, at the time of his wife's death, he wrote concerning it, "Who can contemplate the fact of it and not call the world irrational, if out of deference to a few particles of disorganized matter, it excludes so fair a spirit?"[3]

Does it make sense to think that Antonio Stradivari would

go to all the trouble to make a violin as nearly perfect as human hands can make it, only to take it back after someone has played a few measures on it and smash it to pieces against his workbench? Does it seem right to think that God would create a human life with all its possibilities for wisdom, faith, love, and courage, only to take it back after a brief and inconclusive performance and smash it forever against the workbench of the universe? What would seem to be unreasonable action on the part of a maker of violins would certainly be unthinkable as a course of action for the creator of souls. Surely God is not in the business of preserving atoms and destroying souls. Jesus did not think so. He taught that a living soul is worth more than all the atoms in the world. "What is a man profited," he asked, "if he shall gain the whole world, and lose his own soul?" (Matt. 16:26). Indeed, why worry about saving the soul if it is lost by extinction at death anyhow?

The Bible does not argue the case for eternal life. The Bible assumes it and presents analogies that are like picture windows of faith through which we can look to see something of the promise of eternity, and through which God's eternal sunlight can shine into our own hearts. There is the window of the twenty-third Psalm through which probably more people have looked than any other passage of Scripture. Here death is presented as a passageway, not a stopping place—a passageway that leads to our eternal home.

There are Jesus' comforting words in the fourteenth chapter of John: "Let not your heart be troubled: ye believe in God, believe also in me. In my Father's house are many mansions: if it were not so, I would have told you. I go to prepare a place for you" (vv. 1–2). Jesus began his life in this world in the home of a carpenter. How often, as a youth, he must have helped Joseph build a house for some neighbor. Perhaps it was an actual case Jesus was recalling to mind when he said,

"Which of you, intending to build a tower, sitteth not down first, and counteth the cost, whether he have sufficient to finish it? Lest haply, after he hath laid the foundation, and is not able to finish it, all that behold it begin to mock him" (Luke 14:28–29). How natural, therefore, that as Jesus spoke of heaven, he should have used the analogy of building. We do not know what the mansions of heaven are like, but if he is their architect, we can know their beauty is unsurpassed.

There is Paul's interesting figure in the fifteenth chapter of 1 Corinthians. "Some man," he says, "will say, How are the dead raised up? and with what body do they come?" (v. 35). This is his answer. "That which thou sowest is not quickened, except it die: And that which thou sowest, thou sowest not that body that shall be, but bare grain, it may chance of wheat, or of some other grain: But God giveth it a body as it hath pleased him, and to every seed his own body. . . . So also is the resurrection of the dead" (vv. 36–38, 42). In other words, when we put a seed into the ground, we put not one thing but two. We put the body of the seed that we can see. That part dies as it becomes one with the soil. Inside the part we can see, however, there is the life that we cannot see. That part does not die. Instead, God gives it a new body in the plant, the flower, and the fruit. The God who can do this in the vegetable world, says Paul, can do a similar thing for human life. "It is sown a natural body; it is raised a spiritual body. There is a natural body, and there is a spiritual body. . . . as we have borne the image of the earthy, we shall also bear the image of the heavenly" (vv. 44–49).

There is the striking vision of John in the twenty-first chapter of Revelation: "I saw a new heaven and a new earth: for the first heaven and the first earth were passed away; and there was no more sea" (v. 1). We can hardly imagine what it meant to John to say those words, "and there was no more sea." John was living in exile on the little island of Patmos.

He had been placed there by the Roman authorities for refusing to worship the emperor. All around him was the Mediterranean Sea. He was shut off from the rest of the world by a vast, extending tide of surging ocean. Unless he recanted his faith—which he would never do—John would be separated from his loved ones and friends by this vast, impassable barrier for the rest of his life. There was one thing, however, that Rome with all its power could not do. It could not separate him from his loved ones and beloved Christian friends in heaven. There would be no sea to divide them any more. As the physical heavens and earth receded from his view and spiritual realms took their place in his vision, the first thing he noticed was, "there was no more sea." Instead of separation there would be reunion in a setting so lovely that it could be compared to a bride dressed in shimmering beauty for her wedding.

But the Christian faith in eternal life is not based on mere inference or analogy. It has a more solid foundation that that. It is based on the resurrection of its Lord. One cannot account for the Christian church apart from the resurrection of Jesus. It was not his teachings or his influence—as strong as those must have been in the lives of the disciples—that sent them out to die for their faith. It was their confidence that Jesus was alive again, and would live forevermore. The resurrection turned their discouragement into faith and their despair into victory. "Ye men of Israel," cried Peter, "hear these words; Jesus of Nazareth, a man approved of God among you . . . ye have taken, and by wicked hands have crucified and slain: Whom God hath raised up, having loosed the pains of death: because it was not possible that he should be holden of it" (Acts 2:22–24).

This was their confidence. This was their message. This was their faith. At first it had seemed even to them more than human credulity could accept. To the disciples, the first witness of the women concerning the resurrection seemed "as idle tales, and they believed them not" (Luke 24:11). Then strange things began to happen in their experience. Soon they were convinced, beyond all their human inclination to disbelieve that such a thing could happen, that it was true. Christ was risen. They were confronted by the evidence of the empty tomb. Peter's companion, presumably John, was convinced by the position of the grave clothes. Seeing the way they lay in the tomb, he "saw, and believed" (John 20:8). Others believed as Christ appeared in their midst. Thomas, the hardest of all to convince, was led to cry in faith, "My Lord and my God" (John 20:28).

Christ is risen! This was the truth they went forth to declare. Men do not give their lives for a lie. They do not face martyrdom with tongue in cheek. Whether we believe in Jesus' resurrection or not, the disciples certainly did. The very unanimity of their witness is convincing. Conceivably, one of them could have had a hallucination. It is possible, though hardly probable, that two could have experienced the same delusion. It is beyond all reason, however, to think that eleven men could all experience an identical hallucination. G. D. Yarnold says:

If a number of witnesses can truthfully claim to have shared in a single experience . . . is there not a strong priority case for supposing the objectivity of what is experienced? It is possible for the skeptic to hold that a number of people assembled together could jointly undergo the same spiritual experience, without the occurence of any objective event as of necessity; but only if he admits the existence of a spiritual presence so powerful as to weld their several inner experiences into one. And this surely is tantamount to the admission of the central fact of the presence in their midst of the Risen Lord in a very real sense.[4]

What Paul says of immortality is true of the resurrection: "Behold, I shew you a mystery" (1 Cor. 15:51). As an event, it so far transcends our human understanding as to defy all attempts to explain it. But neither, in the light of its consequences in the lives of the disciples and the subsequent life of the church, can any one succeed in fully explaining it away.

But does it matter whether or not we believe in immortality? Harry Emerson Fosdick says it matters very much. For one thing, our whole concept of the power and goodness of God is tied up with it. "A just and fatherly God," says Fosdick, "cannot have brought into being children, capable of endless growth, aspiring after knowledge and character, only to toss them one by one into oblivion . . . As the seers have always felt, the goodness and honor of God are at stake in the question of immortality." [5] If God cannot cause immortality to happen, he is not God. If he can but will not, he is not the God we see in Jesus Christ. Indeed, Leslie Weatherhead contends that the two chief reasons for believing in life after death are: first, the character of God—if God is like Jesus, he would not taunt us by creating in us the desire for eternal life, only to deny it to us in the end—and second, the trustworthiness of Jesus. If immortality is not possible or true, Jesus would not have promised it. God is a Father who wants the best for his children. The best we can conceive is that they shall have eternal life.

It is God's goodness that gives us hope to believe this. "While a man . . . may believe in immortality without believing in the goodness of God," says Fosdick, "he cannot reasonably believe in the goodness of God without believing in immortality." [6] But goodness cannot operate in a vacuum. If one is good, his actions must show it in the way he deals with others. Even God cannot be a God of justice and love without being just and loving toward someone. Is he righteous only to those who are now alive? Is his love limited to those who now walk this earth? It is his love and justice, in fact, that require that there shall be life after death, so that those who are denied love and justice in this world may experience it in the life to come. "Without immortality," says Fosdick, "the long struggle of humanity has no consummation in which harmony comes at last out of the present discord of inequity." [7]

Again, the doctrine of immortality is an affirmation of the eternal worth of character, an affirmation "which alone can make reasonable the devotion, aspiration, and self-denial which great character requires." [8] We have asked whether Stradivari would create a masterpiece only to destroy it after it had been played a few times. Let us turn the illustration around and ask whether, if he knew it was going to be destroyed after it had been played a few times, he would feel like putting all his skill and energy into making it a masterpiece. As Fosdick so strikingly puts it:

Does Ictinus pick out a quicksand on which to build the Parthenon and lavish on it there the genius of his art, knowing that every stroke of his mallet is making a beauty that today is and tomorrow will be gone? Does Raphael choose cotton cloth, whose slender and loosely woven fibers will hardly bear the strokes of his brush, on which to paint a Sistine Madonna? And will a man develop passionate moral enthusiasms and aspiring virtues on any other basis than spiritual permanence? [9]

It is the thought of immortality that gives man his greatest incentive for high moral endeavor. Paul brings this out clearly when he says, "If in this life only we have hope in Christ, we are of all men most miserable. But now is Christ risen from the dead, and become the firstfruits of them that slept. . . . Therefore, . . . be ye stedfast, unmoveable, always abounding in the work of the Lord, forasmuch as ye know that your labour is not in vain in the Lord" (1 Cor. 15:19–20, 58). This is our greatest incentive for noble living—the confidence that our faith in and service for Christ are not in vain. In the life to come, they are brought to the perfect fulfilment that eludes us in this life.

In Washington, D. C., there is a musical group known as the Budapest String Quartet. It is made up of four highly skilled musicians who each year present a series of concerts in the Coolidge Auditorium of the Library of Congress. At these concerts, each plays on a priceless Stradivarius instrument. The players do not own these instruments. They are the property of the Library of Congress. At the conclusion of the concert season, the instruments are turned over to the proper custodian who places them for protection in a hermetically sealed vault where they are kept at the right temperature and humidity to preserve their tonal quality. Thus they are preserved for generations to come, so that music lovers yet unborn may be able to enjoy their tone.

Human existence is not a cheap instrument to be discarded when life's concert is over. Each living being is a masterpiece to be returned to God's hands who alone is able to preserve it for eternity. Life is not ours to do with as we please. It is to be held in sacred trust that we may give it back to its rightful owner who can fit it into his eternal plan. We must not, by indifference or rejection, permit it to become so warped with self-will and sin that it cannot resound with a song of faith and love either in this world or the next.

The very fact that men desire eternal life is an argument for its existence. Is thirst not an indication that God has provided water for its quenching? Is hunger not a sign that he has provided food? Can man outthink God? "I will not believe," said Sir Oliver Lodge, "that it is given to man to have thoughts nobler or loftier than the real truth of things." [10] And Leslie Weatherhead says that when you are thinking about God, you cannot wish better than the truth.[11] Does not the fact that in our best moments we are dissatisfied with ourselves, are left unsatisfied by earth's blessings, and long for a heaven in which to know perfect fulfilment indicate that God has planned to provide it?

Faith in eternal life lifts life to new levels of joy and significance. This being true, it is better to live as if eternal life were true, even if death proves us to be wrong, than to live as if there were no God, no life after death, no judgment, and then to find out we were wrong.

This cannot be said too strongly. If immortality is true, it is not something to be taken lightly. Perhaps that, after all, is our greatest problem. It is not so much that men disbelieve in life after death, but that so many take its possibility so casually. "We have come," says Samuel H. Miller, "to feel very tolerant and comfortable, as though every soul, regardless of its self-neglect or self-destructiveness, will come at last to have heaven dropped in its undeserving hands. This belief is not in the New Testament." [12] How can we deny the spiritual a place in our lives and expect to enjoy it after death? How can we deny God our love in life and expect it to make no difference to him in the life to come? He promises to build us a "house not made with hands, eternal in the heavens" (2 Cor. 5:1), but what if we do not hold the key of faith that unlocks its door?

The Bible shows us the way that leads to eternal life. It does not present a set of rules and say, "Do this, and this, and this, and you will inherit eternal life." It presents Jesus and says, "Follow him. He came from God; he will lead you to God." He is our greatest assurance that eternal life is true. It was Jesus who said, "My sheep hear my voice, and I know them, and they follow me: And I give unto them eternal life; and they shall never perish, neither shall any man pluck them out of my hand" (John 10:27–28). Of this he was confident because his life was held in a larger plan. "My Father, which gave them me, is greater than all; and no man is able to pluck them out of my Father's hand" (John 10:29). And there is no danger of the hands coming apart: "I and my Father are one" (John 10:30). This is the faith that overflows into eternal life.

Notes

Introduction

1. *The Country of the Pointed Firs and Other Stories* (Garden City, N. Y.: Doubleday & Co., Inc., 1956), p. 84.

2. *The Bible Speaks to You* (Philadelphia: The Westminster Press, 1955), pp. 24–25.

Chapter 1

1. From *Rudyard Kipling's Verse, Definitive Edition.* Reprinted by permission of Mrs. George Bambridge and Doubleday & Co., Inc.

2. Rufus M. Jones, *The Radiant Life* (New York: The Macmillan Co., 1944), p. 6.

3. "Service," *1000 Quotable Poems* (Chicago: Willett, Clark & Co., 1937), I, 73.

4. *Beliefs That Matter* (New York: Charles Scribner's Sons, 1928), p. 152.

5. *I and Thou* (New York: Charles Scribner's Sons, 1957), p. 112.

Chapter 2

1. Jones, *op. cit.*, p. 3.

2. Quoted in Margueritte Bro, *More Than We Are* (New York: Harper & Bros., 1948), pp. 7–8.

3. *Ibid.*, p. 24.

4. *Ibid.*, p. 29.

5. Yokefellow Associates, Earlham College, Richmond, Indiana.

6. *The Practice of the Presence of God* (New York: Fleming H. Revell Co., 1895), Eighth Letter, p. 36.

7. *Strengthening the Spiritual Life* (New York: Harper & Bros., 1951), p. 15.

8. *Op. cit.*, Seventh Letter, pp. 34–35.

9. *The Dazzling Darkness* (New York: Longmans, Green & Co., 1950), p. 39.

Chapter 3

1. *The Text of the Spiritual Exercises of Saint Ignatius* (Westminster, Md.: Newman Bookshop, n.d.), p. 1.

2. *Adventuring in Prayer* (Philadelphia: The Westminster Press, 1942).

3. *Prayer, the Mightiest Force in the World* (New York: Fleming H. Revell Co., 1946), chapter 4.

4. Ferré, *op. cit.*, p. 13.

5. *The Life of the Soul* (New York: Harper & Bros., 1951), pp. 82, 84.

6. *Creative Prayer* (New York: Harper & Bros., 1934), p. 40.

7. Miller, *op. cit.*, p. 84.

8. *Op. cit.*, p. 30.

9. *Op. cit.*, p. 35.

10. *The Poems of Sidney Lanier* (New York: Charles Scribner's Sons, 1891), p. 17.

11. Quoted in Edward W. Bauman, *Intercessory Prayer* (Philadelphia: The Westminster Press, 1958), p. 22.

12. *Preaching the Gospel of the Resurrection* (Philadelphia: The Westminster Press, 1954), p. 32.

13. Miller, *op. cit.*, p. 69.

14. *Ibid.*, p. 107.

15. *A Shepherd Remembers* (New York: Abingdon Press, 1938), p. 129.

16. *Op. cit.*, p. 35.

17. *The Nature of the Physical World* (New York: The Macmillan Co., 1928), p. 342.

18. Bauman, *op. cit.*, p. 32.

Chapter 4

1. "The Search," *1000 Quotable Poems, op. cit.*, I, 162.

2. Quoted in Hans Hofmann (ed.), *Making the Ministry Relevant* (New York: Charles Scribner's Sons, 1960), p. 25.

3. Joseph Belcher, *William Carey* (Philadelphia: American Baptist Publication Society, 1853), pp. 122–23.

4. *Op. cit.*, p. 88.

5. Hofmann, *op. cit.*, p. 23.

6. *The Psychology of Christian Personality* (New York: The Macmillan Co., 1935), p. 152.

Chapter 5

1. *Op. cit.*, p. 64.
2. Belcher, *op. cit.*, p. 243.
3. *Ibid.*, pp. 18–19.
4. *Ibid.*, pp. 61–62.
5. *Ibid.*, p. 136.
6. *Thomas A. Edison, a Modern Olympian* (New York: Harrison Smith & Robert Haas, 1934), p. 77.
7. *Op. cit.*, pp. 125 ff.
8. *Psychology and Morals* (New York: Robert McBride & Co., 1933), p. 112.
9. *Spiritual Renewal Through Personal Groups* (New York: Association Press, 1957), p. 19.
10. *Ibid.*, p. 22.
11. S. E. Frost (ed.), *The World's Greatest Sermons* (Garden City, N. Y.: Halcyon House, 1943), p. 133.
12. Bowden, *op. cit.*, p. 22.

Chapter 6

1. *The Character of Jesus* (New York: Grosset & Dunlap, 1936), p. 18.

Chapter 7

1. *Spirit, Son and Father* (New York: Charles Scribner's Sons, 1959), p. 90.
2. *Ibid.*, p. viii.
3. (London: Nisbet & Co., 1936), p. 4.
4. "The Messenger," (Washington, D.C.: Metropolitan Memorial Methodist Church), April, 1963.
5. *The Holy Spirit in Christian Theology* (Philadelphia: The Westminster Press, 1956), p. 26.
6. *The Holy Spirit, Who He Is, and What He Does* (New York: Fleming H. Revell Co., 1927), p. 14.
7. *Op. cit.*, p. 18.
8. *Ibid.*, pp. 175–76.
9. *The Resurrection of Christ* (Philadelphia: The Westminster Press, 1946), p. 10.
10. *Op. cit.*, p. 118.

Chapter 8

1. *The Gospel in Dispute* (Garden City, N. Y.: Doubleday & Co., Inc., 1958), p. 4.

2. *Op. cit.*, p. 43.

3. *Op. cit.*, p. 165.

4. *The Student Faces Life* (Philadelphia: Judson Press, 1932), p. 99.

5. *The Complete Poetry and Selected Prose of John Donne*, ed. Charles M. Coffin (New York: The Modern Library, 1952), pp. 525–26.

6. *Op. cit.*, Eighth Letter, p. 35.

7. *Op. cit.*, p. 60.

Chapter 9

1. *Op. cit.*, p. 50.

2. *Op. cit.*, p. 20.

3. First published by Stratford Co. and used by Simon & Schuster in *Outposts of Science*, p. 159.

4. *Christianity and the New World* (New York: Harper & Bros., 1932), p. 16.

Chapter 10

1. *The World's Need of Christ* (New York: Abingdon-Cokesbury Press, 1940), p. 23.

2. *The Assurance of Immortality* (New York: Association Press, 1931), p. 8.

3. *Ibid.*, p. 8.

4. *Risen Indeed* (Fair Lawn, N. J.: Oxford University Press, 1959), p. 4.

5. *Op. cit.*, p. 94.

6. *Ibid.*, p. 102.

7. *Ibid.*, p. 33.

8. *Ibid.*, p. 31.

9. *Ibid.*

10. *Ibid.*, p. 18.

11. *The Resurrection and the Life* (New York: Abingdon Press, 1952), p. 44.

12. *Op. cit.*, p. 152.

Date Due